Go In Joy!

An Alphabetical Adventure

Joy Resor

Go In Joy! An Alphabetical Adventure
by Joy Resor

Second Edition

Joy On Your Shoulders
P.O. Box 951
Pisgah Forest, NC 28768

Find Joy on the Web at: joyonyourshoulders.com

A version of *A Message Arrives in Stereo* appears as *A Friend's Just-Right Response* in *365 Soulful Messages: The Right Guidance at the Right Time* by Jodi Chapman, Dan Teck & Over 200 Soulful Contributors, 2019.

A version of *Girlfriends* appears in Confluence, Volume 17, 2006.

A version of *Letter to My Workshop Leader* appears in *Tributaries*, Issue 5, 2002.

ISBN: 978-0-9840353-7-3

Advance Praise

"What does this book feel like? Turning these pages is like walking into a surprise party given to celebrate me, personal attention that in my private heart I usually resist, but here, with the verve, ease and spirit of this book by Joy Resor, I am won over. There is an immediacy in my sense of surprise – Resor's writing style is one of engagement. *Go in Joy! An Alphabetical Adventure* deftly weaves together rich stories, keen reflections, beautiful and provocative questions along with poems that get to the heart and bone of the matter: how you can live your life and be in relationship with more honesty, greater joy and an unequivocal authenticity."

—John Fox; *Finding What You Didn't Lose: Expressing Your Truth and Creativity Through Poem-Making 20th anniversary*

"GO IN JOY! is a wonderfully delightful book that leaves us wanting more. It's full of profound questions skillfully wrapped in colorful leaves of innocence and playfulness. Sometimes "clever" can be overdone. Not here. The author's inventive weaving of words is brilliant. A charming and healing read."

—Dr. Suka Chapel-Horst; *Take a Leap of Faith*

"This wonderful collection of delicious, bite-sized essays are ideal readings to reflect on as you start or end your day. Joy takes us into her heart and along the pathway of her own spiritual journey, from wounding, confusion and self-doubt into a full engagement and celebration of all aspects of life, shadow and light. Lyrical and inspiring, it is filled with the gems of wisdom she has gathered along the way."

—Chelsea Wakefield; *Negotiating the Inner Peace Treaty*

I dedicate this book to YOU, dear reader.

And I dedicate this book to Loving Life, and to the human/ spiritual trapeze on which we balance.

Also By Joy Resor:

Venture to Your Center—Journaling Prompts to Enliven Your Joy

Designed to SHINE! Read Aloud Rhymes for Any Size Heart

Contents

Foreword

It is June 1st, and I sit on my porch in Flat Rock, North Carolina basking in the beauty of nature, and feeling so much gratitude for all of the blessings in my life. I also am grateful for the opportunity to share with you the gift of this fantastic book written by Joy. I just finished reading *Go In Joy! An Alphabetical Adventure*-...and yes it is! It is *all* about expanding our JOY, and for sure an adventure!

In today's world, souls feel challenged in so many ways. Life has become difficult and the joy in life seems as though it has been lost. The good news is that there is a way back to living a happier, healthy and meaningful life, assisted by the support of this joyful book.

I have had the blessing and opportunity to spend time with Joy. The words of wisdom she shares on the following pages are more than whimsical new age musings. They are straight from the heart of a woman who has turned her life completely around.

Joy writes from personal experience. She shares facets of despair and suffering as well as ways to transform life from fear to love. *Go In Joy!* is everyone's story. Maybe the experiences we've had are not the same as Joy's, but the feelings of sadness, not being heard, living a lie and not being true to ourselves are relatable for us all.

The great news is that Joy offers us a gentle path back to find our bliss! There are questions to answer, beautiful poetry to ponder, and most importantly, the tale of a woman who speaks from experience.

I continue to be in awe of Joy's transformation into the love she freely offers with so many. I know you will be touched by this book as I have.

Blessings to each of you on your journey.

Peace and Love Prevail on Earth! And So It Is!

Namaste,
Rev. Charlotte McGinnis
Flat Rock, North Carolina

Introduction

Are we offering ourselves in the world with energy matching our desires?

When people meet us, do they walk away feeling better?

I'm honored to write this book, because aspects of my journey may speak to you in ways that increase your energy or enliven your joy.

When we meet, people ask if my given name is Joy, or if I chose it, because they feel joyful energy in my presence. I reply that it's my given name I've been led to heal into, which makes them smile. Then they typically say they want what I have.

I understand, because for many decades, I sought this version of myself, too…Joy with an open heart and a playful, welcoming spirit, the woman radiating enough peace to fill any room to the ceiling and beyond.

I'm humbled and grateful to offer *Go In Joy! An*

Alphabetical Adventure to add joy to your life through stories, treasures and surprises. *Go In Joy!* is designed to literally be read from A to Z, or by jumping in where you're ready to engage; any order you select is just right.

You'll discover snippets of my suffering, recovery tips and tales of expanding our consciousness, as I heal from constricted, scared, perfectionistic tendencies into allowing, appreciating and loving practices, living more fully into each moment.

You'll meet members of my dear family of origin. You'll encounter Dad's raging, Mom's perfectionism, and my sister's litany that I don't belong. You'll meet crying me running from the table, contemplative me on a rock and forgiving me centered in loving acceptance.

You'll meet dear men in my life I'll call Wally, Ben, Dan and Michael. Wally is my former husband, or "wasbund," a telling moniker a friend mentioned, and father to our grown sons. Ben enters when our marriage ends, then Dapper Dan with a joyful vibration, followed by Michael, co-adventuring with me in the unlimited field of possibilities.

And you'll meet our family dog I'll call Spice, remembered for years of surprises, excitement and love.

Questions and invitations to discover our healing edges are embedded throughout *Go In Joy! An Alphabetical Adventure.* And in this, its second edition, you'll find fresh poems and essays to enliven your joy; I've had a delight writing while loving life since this book was first published in 2015; later this year, book number four will be published.

My deepest longing is that this story of emerging through life's traumas inspires all of us into a journey of expanding our joy as we more deeply love our lives.

To all the Love, Peace and Joy we can be and share.

Blessings on your journey,

Joy
www.joyonyourshoulders.com

P.S. Invite friends to read and discuss *An Alphabetical Adventure* with you. Contact joy@joyonyourshoulders.com to purchase multiple copies at a good price of this highly relatable book that groups enjoy sharing.

Chapter A

Might We Adventure Beyond Old Limits?

Is it time to stretch beyond a comfort zone?
If we breathe into possibilities, what will arise?
What does your heart long to do?

Sharing a summer call with my son who is in the Peace Corps in Namibia, I surprise myself when this question escapes my lips.

"Would you like me to visit?"

"Of course, Mom! And let's go on a photo safari."

Wow.

What did I just propose?

There was a time I wouldn't leave the house without checking the locks twice, and here I am acting like it's nothing to travel across the world.

Andrew requests leave, I meet with Toby of Outdoor Africa and a plan is in motion for March 2017.

Time moves along.

A friend asks, "What camera are you taking to Africa in two weeks, Joy?"

What?!

Maybe you have experienced this, too—living moment by moment, events in an imagined future meet us before we know it.

Returning home, I focus on equipment, attire and the fact that *I really* am going on an incredible adventure, very soon.

Yes!

Even though this is WAY out of my zone of experiences.

I fly fifteen hours from Atlanta to Johannesburg with noise-canceling headphones, snacks and excitement for time with my son, reflecting on this rare occurrence.

How many parents get this chance?

Andrew is thirty-two-years-old, single and open to being WITH me for over two weeks, and I have the ability, means and interest to share with him.

Our photo safari and visit in Swakopmund, Namibia are beautiful, HOT, overflowing with animal sightings, great food and laughter.

I still pinch myself; I'm unbelievably grateful that I leaned into adventure.

I've been on a long journey to unwind tight tendencies that kept me scared, compacted, watching life from a safe distance.

Reflecting on the last decade, it's clear that I'm not the fearful, risk-adverse girl/woman I've been for eons.

I'm beyond a zillion fearful thoughts, and I'm happier, freer and more connected to others than before.

Hooray!

I see this for YOU, dear reader.

I believe in your growth beyond all that holds you back from becoming your radiant, amazing, adventuring Self.

Lean past limits into an adventure!

Alignment Must Be Nirvana

When we hear the word ***alignment,*** *what comes to mind?*

Our car's tires?

I understand.

What else?

Anything?

Spiritual alignment?

Great! You'll find that topic in the essay *What Separation is Ours to Heal?* in Chapter S.

How about this?

Do you remember walking with a book on your head as a child?

A focus back in the day was for us to have good posture, wasn't it?

Body alignment is related to that.

It's about how our heads sit on our spines and on down…how our bodies are lined up or out of line, which affects how we walk, how we sit, how we stand and how much ease, injury or pain we may be in, as well.

I'm rather new to understanding much about alignment, but I'm all for it.

I'm in favor of being an aligned person these days, that's for sure.

Here's a bit of the tale, starting with a scene from fifteen years ago.

Attempting to wrap my arms around the woman next to me in our closing circle, I return them to the front, saying, "I can't. Can we hold hands instead?"

Afterward, a nearby woman curtly says, "Your chest is tight."

Hmm…that isn't a gentle way to let me know, and what do I do about that, I wonder? Is this chest tightness related to Mom's curve in her upper spine and Grandma's Dowager's Hump?

Taking Pilates years later, the word alignment arises, newly waking me to the fact that my frame leans towards the opposite…compacted.

I grew up in a loving and fear-based home where Dad's angry outbursts sent me to my room into a crying ball under the covers hugging Chessie, my stuffed cat. Bless Dad's wounded heart, yelling at us for small infractions—falling down, talking when the news is on and playing too loudly when he's reading the paper.

Does this sound familiar?

Was your household hostage to unexpected whims of anger?

Would peace rock off its hinges by slammed doors?

Did you nurse legions of hurt feelings?

Fear also rings my bell as a latch-key child imagining the Boogeyman jumping out of the bushes to grab me when I come home alone from school, or while we watch the movie, *The Birds*, as I peek through my fingers at the Magnavox with my head nestled into the couch.

As a young mother, my car is rear-ended and totaled, giving me neck and back soft tissue injuries, along with fear driving where I've never been.

When the Towers are attacked in 2001, a new layer of fearful thoughts gets stuck inside, particularly around flying.

Contraction. Fear.

Life appears scary, until my husband and I prepare to move from Ohio to the mountains of western North Carolina when I evolve into viewing the future in a positive way instead of with fear. A year after we're in the mountains, as I move for the third time in eighteen months heading for divorce, I begin viewing life in completely new ways.

This is typical, as I understand it, because when forms around us disappear or shift in a flash through natural disasters, multiple family deaths, divorce and more, we release layers of fear, layers of ego and layers of control. We begin to see life changing as the way life is.

Life Equals Change

Bring on change! Bring on a new place for me to live. I can pack up and move, portable me. How cool is it to rent instead of own?

Freedom!

What if I decide to change from a compacted person to an aligned person?

It must be possible.

What if I begin to believe...that I become aligned in my frame…that I become a woman in my family without a Dowager's Hump…that I stand tall for my shorter frame…that when I'm aligned, the energy of the Universe flows through me?

If I believe I become aligned, I'll go to massage, to the Chiropractor, to Rolfing and to Pilates.

I'll watch my body shift from compacted to open and aligned.

Consider better alignment to advance your joy.

Of Childhood Fears and a Hero

I

Alone in the tiled kitchen on silent feet,
I pack my paper sack the same each morning—
half a jelly sandwich, Twinkie, bag of chips.
After school, I fish the house key from my blouse
as fear nibbles, slip into a silent house, lock the door.

Rainy days, purple pink worms long as braids
line the street like parade watchers.
I try not to squash any,
cast a song into worm-scented air,
Whenever I feel afraid, I hold my head erect…

II

I climb Uncle Hank's ample lap, tuck my face
into his sweatered chest where the best view waits.
Any minute he'll pop his false teeth out, then in,
send my *wow* to the corner and back for a fresh
carton of Nik'l Nip and a pack of Beatles cards.

His denture trickery is our secret handshake,
code of entry, the key to a treasure chest.
Once a year, I endure carsick miles
through three states to nestle into Hank's waiting lap,
reeling in a prize-winning catch
of connection.

If We Allow a Little More…

Admittedly, the concept of allowing is newer for me.

I come from a dear line of perfectionists and controlling souls who aren't big fans; they want things a particular way.

Truth be told, they create lots of drama which gives me emotional pain, the part of my journey calling me into the peace and joy I radiate.

My parents aren't healed into whole, serene beings, coming from parents who aren't healed into whole, serene beings and on through our ancestral lineage.

Can you relate?

Are you an adult who grew up in a home of mood swings and unpredictability?

Allowing each person to be who he or she is in any moment is a gift to everyone present. In a sense, we're witnessing the other or holding space for the other to be who they are.

Allowing invites freedom into moments, which brings us to acceptance.

The more I accept and love myself, the more I'm able to accept and love you, allowing you to be who you are.

Here's an event in our lives which brings this idea into focus.

Ben and I head out on a sunny October Sunday to walk a trail, discovering crowded roads without a parking space.

When Ben complains, I breathe and smile, mentioning that it is a gorgeous Sunday in October, so many people have the same plan.

Ben continues to be upset, and I continue to breathe and smile, taking in the blue sky, the shades of yellow, orange and red, realizing that my mood doesn't need to change just because Ben feels agitated, progress from my co-dependent past.

Arriving at another forest to hike, I notice that instead of taking my hand in his to match our usual pattern stepping onto the trail, Ben charges ahead, clearly in his process, perhaps angry with himself.

I consider that an earlier version of me may have told him to cut it out, or a tape in mind from childhood could have run so that my mood became dark as well.

But I am who I am any given moment, as we all are. This sunny afternoon in autumn, I enjoy the trail, the colors and myself, allowing this dear soul to feel how he feels without entering his experience.

Grating carrots into dinner salads, I reflect.

"We don't need Ben's garbage in our lives," my ego admonishes.

I respond that Ben is a wonderful man who happens to be human; we can allow him to be himself, with his growth, his journey and his garbage.

Without getting high on myself, I admit within that I'm grateful I've grown enough to sometimes allow souls to be who they are, even if they're feeling rather off. It feels like a bit of a coup for someone who simmered long in a cauldron of colorful, co-dependent soup.

And questions arise…

How often do we allow life to be what it is, without needing it to be otherwise, without resisting what it is, by simply accepting the moment before us?

When we're driving along and we encounter a traffic jam, how do we react or respond? Do we get all tense and angry? Do we breathe and stretch? Do we pray the jam swiftly clears? Do we make a call? Have we left extra time to arrive where we're heading? Are we running late again?

I've evolved from reacting as my family did to leaving extra time, allowing me to respond with a smile, knowing that the jam will clear, because I'm usually not trying to cram too many stops into my days.

For the most part, I no longer run on adrenalin. I breathe into moments, activity and appointments, allowing life to unfold with ease and grace, as it does so well.

Live into more allowing with others and moments.

Honoring Our Ancestors

How often do we consider our ancestors?
Do we regularly send and receive love?
Is it time to honor our ancestors more often?

At the Southern Appalachian Dowsers Conference, Dan visits a Native American Medicine Woman/ Shaman who offers a powerful reading. Returning to the *Joy on Your Shoulders* booth, he says, "Go see this reader; she's wondrous."

"Sure!"

I highly resonate with referrals. Do you?

My reading with Patricia astounds me with its accuracy.

She says the book I'm writing is magic in the world, and that a block to bringing it forward involves my ancestors, who ache to guide this book into being. Patricia tells me to create an altar honoring them, communing each morning and evening.

I share that I received a knowing a few months earlier to create an ancestral altar, though I haven't followed through.

When I reunite with Dan, and as I begin to recall the reading, my ancestors start pummeling me with love.

"Dan, how do I receive all of this energy?"

"Put it into your heart, darling."

And I do...until it becomes challenging to receive the amount of LOVE entering, so Dan guides me to a treatment table in the back of the hall where I can lie down.

After my ancestors have finished, all the ancestors of the earth line up to put love into my heart.

In a flash, my hearing becomes so acute that I can't stand to stay inside, so Dan leads me to a quiet bench beside a pond.

When I'm able to function in a more normal fashion, I see each person with a loving gaze that begins in my heart.

Blessings to you, to as much love as you can be and share and to your beloved ancestors, dear one.

May we honor our ancestors with loving intention.

Answering Machines and Machinations

Are we early adopters of new gadgets?

Do we ride the leading edge to own the latest iPhone?

Do we move more slowly adapting to technology?

As a young Mom writing the church newsletter, my friends start to grouse when they have trouble reaching me.

"Joy, I needed to leave you a message!"

"Buy an answering machine, Joy!"

Sigh. Yes, I am a late bloomer in many ways, including the adaptation of popular, newfangled (back in the 80s) conveniences like answering machines.

Making my friends happy, I finally get one.

Later, we have voice mail.

I get a flip phone later than most.

I get a smart phone at the end of the curve.

My copy machine makes copies. It doesn't fax. It doesn't scan.

You get the picture.

I don't begrudge early adopters.

It's just not in my make-up.

I'm pleased with owning less.

I'm pleased with machines that do one thing.

Heck, Ben and I actually live together six months before buying a dryer, a decision reached when I no longer will freeze my fingers off hanging laundry on the glass-enclosed porch in February.

Plus, there's a complication, which is why our landlord didn't leave us with one in the first place; the doorway to the laundry room is narrower than typical dryers.

Come to think of it, I can be years behind on lots of things. Today, I'm reading a shady book everyone read nine years ago.

Acquire goods on your time table.

Enough

When we stop eating
Before fullness

Turn off devices
Hours before sleep

Take pressure off
Ourselves

To be more than
We are

Gifts
Arise
From
Our depths.

Where's Our Attention?

Where our attention is focused highly matters.

When you're reading this, are your mind and heart right here?

Other times, is your attention focused on your task, or do you do one thing, say driving, while your attention is elsewhere?

You arrive at your destination on auto pilot—with no memory of the drive.

I imagine we've all done this and more…maneuver through days with our bodies and minds in two different places.

Growing up, I feel my family isn't seeing me.

They look toward me with distracted minds; they aren't giving me a fullness of attention my authentic self desires.

In time, I grow into my own active mind, a person who sees you but doesn't truly see you. Though we may not have liked some of our upbringing, our upbringing becomes us…go figure.

What behaviors do we see in ourselves that we don't enjoy in others?

Can we tweak a pattern to act in a new way?

A classic book to guide us into a more mindful way of being in the world is by Jon Kabat-Zinn, *Wherever You Go There You Are.* In short essays, Zinn leads us into increasingly conscious ways to experience life.

I love this book. Every couple of years, I pull it off the shelf to re-enter Zinn's approach, and now and then, I loan it to a friend.

Hooray! Practicing mindfulness for a few years, my mind has quieted. It's amazing what I notice. Washing my hair in the shower, loose strands skim my behind and calves on their way down, a subtle feeling that surprises my awareness.

Address one task at a time.

B

Chapter B

Balance on Deck

What an interesting section title arises, since I'm prone to seasickness…argh.

How do you and boats rock?

Balance leads me to consider seesaws, balance beams and old time scales.

Balance.

Have we all been or known someone suffering with a balance issue from too much alcohol or from an inner ear or other malady?

Then there's our work and relaxing balance to consider.

Overwork, anyone?

How much balance do we navigate?

Socializing and being by ourselves—different for introverts and extroverts.

Introverts can become unbalanced holding too many conversations or being with too many people in a day, energetically wiping us out, until we return to a semblance of balance.

Extroverts process life differently, gaining energy by talking and being with others. I understand alone time sometimes leads to boredom for you.

Dear extrovert, do you feel a pull to balance your energies like introverts do?

How does it look for you?

If I'm at the computer too long, my body craves balance with a stretch, or encourages me to step onto the porch to feel the breeze, receive a sunbeam, or listen to the birds.

When the weather's not welcoming, I balance sitting with a splash of hooping inside.

If I haven't talked with friends in a while, I text to arrange a call.

Before I was in touch with myself in these ways, I could get out of balance…stay up too late…eat too much sugar…do too many errands.

Oh my.

A memory arises, preceding awareness to add balance into my life.

This also is before I am grounded, a topic I write about in Chapter G.

Imagine me as a young mom with long hair…slender, 5' 2 ½"…flitting through the mall during Christmas season carrying too many heavy bags months after my car is totaled, giving me neck and back injuries.

I muse…

My car is parked far away, and these bags are heavy. This isn't helpful for my body, which hurts. Darn! Why did I do this, again? I'll need recovery time…when will I learn not to push the limits of my endurance? Why did I buy so much today?

Ha ha.

I smile, for even though I'm now grounded in my body, and even though I'm awake to caring for myself, life's given me plenty of reminders.

I've carried items that taxed my frame, fallen running for aid and bruised myself reaching for an item as my chair tips over.

Each time, I reflect.

Okay.

I could have done that differently, yet I threw myself out of balance.

Does this sound familiar?

Has this ever been your experience?

Unconscious moments enter to derail our higher understandings, don't they?

Yes.

And I'm a big proponent of not beating myself up. I love myself too much to add blame to unconscious action. Sometimes, I even laugh when I make a silly error.

We are humans, after all—who make mistakes discerning how much we can or cannot do, and lots of other mis-takes.

A goal in life is to be as awake as possible each moment.

Plus, being aware brings us into more Balance with our whole selves.

Awaken to the gifts of balance.

Lesson Plan

Ask your heart to lead
from merry go rounds of action
to the grounding rhythms
it knows in the dark.

There, wisdom lingers
on the edges of each breath,
sending messages on intuition.

And you, wise soul
who spins fragments into balance,
listen.

Balloons, Of Course!

For a smile.

For celebration.

Just the word **balloon** makes me smile.

You, too?

Sometimes, after I finish a task requiring intense effort, I envision streamers, confetti and balloons raining down.

Well…maybe not really.

But I intend to now, because that sounds like a joyful idea, doesn't it?

Popped balloons make me jump, along with any loud noise; you may not want to sit next to me in a movie. Seems my startle reflex long has been on overdrive.

Hot Air Balloon Rides!

Imagine me giving my husband a certificate for a romantic hot air balloon ride at sunset, which he trades in for new golf clubs…

...which gives me a sense of relief, after all...since I'd taken a giant step beyond my comfort of heights to buy it for him.

Do you enjoy batting a balloon over a net?
Bobbing one in the air?
Playing catch with water balloons?

To balloon whimsy!

Beatles Cards and Other Losses

Growing up in the 60s, I love the Beatles.

Specifically Paul.

John is okay.

George and Ringo, not so much.

I also love riding my bike to Gray's Drugstore in Liberty Township north of Youngstown, Ohio, with Dad or a friend on a sunny afternoon to buy packs of Beatles cards. Trading them.

Briefly chewing sugar-dusted pieces of brittle gum enclosed in waxy packs.

Organizing them in a shoe box.

When I am twelve, we move from our ranch house close to town to a larger, contemporary ranch in the suburbs.

In the move, my Beatles cards vanish!

For years, I look into every box in the basement trying to reconstruct how my treasured box of Beatles cards could have disappeared.

Years later, my mind repeatedly catalogs the material losses I've suffered—Beatles cards…J.F.K. half dollars…my yellow jacket with orange and white stripes above the elbows—and something inside me holds onto a sadness about these missing items.

Does your mind inventory losses, too?

But after I move three times in eighteen months, and the marriage I thought would never end, ends, I give up my mind's hold on sadness about Beatles cards and other things that went missing long ago.

Whew.

That's a relief and a half.

Release your mind's hold on lost objects.

What's Our Story of Belonging?

Do we feel we belong in our family?
Have we felt like a wheel that doesn't fit?
Do we feel we belong on the earth?
Have we healed into a comfortable sense of belonging?

If belonging lives as a wound inside us, may we find our way to know how much we belong to ourselves, our lives and on the earth.

We matter.

We truly, truly do!

I understand…believe me, I understand.

Here's how my life begins:

On my due date, I'm born in Maimonides Hospital in Brooklyn, New York, where Mom has been staying with her parents while Dad trains with the Air Force in Georgia. When I am three weeks old, our family moves to Loring Air Force Base in Northern Maine.

My older sister is up all day playing and talking as a bright two-and-a-half-year-old, and I sleep, because 1) I am awake all night communing with the Heavens, 2) my highly sensitive nature needs to tune out big sis and her shenanigans or because 3) I am an infant who simply has her days and nights mixed up.

No matter the reason, Mom starts to feel crazy from exhaustion, so Dad arranges for me to stay for a spell in the Base Hospital Nursery.

Growing up, my sister picks up words Dad utters as a joke, repeatedly sassing this litany at me, "Mom and Dad put you back in the hospital because you cried too much. Then they got the wrong baby back. You really don't belong in our family!"

Ouch!

Over time, even though sis no longer sings this painful fib, the words and meaning have attached to my being—constantly swirling through…I don't belong in this family. I don't belong. I don't belong. I don't belong.

I carry this issue of not belonging in my hip pocket. I don't belong in this nursery school at the church because we're Jewish. I don't belong in this bold, circus-striped dress when every girl at this dance wears pastels.

During my teens, I retreat to my room to doodle with colored markers or to write poetry, finding a measure of peace in my soul.

As a young mother, I don't belong to the neighborhood book group in the intellectual way the circle discusses books. Many months, I can't begin the assigned volume, because an unending list of non-fiction books calls to my healing journey.

Thankfully, in 2011, I receive the gift of belonging.

Have you heard the terms Core Wounds or Root Causes, or is there something that has forever bothered you?

Maybe you feel as though you'll never be enough, for instance. I felt some of that, too.

May you find your way to heal into the understanding that you are more than enough.

May you discover healing through any wound that continues to affect your acceptance of your amazing, unrepeatable self.

I believe that life almost reveals more beauty than we can hold after we heal into loving ourselves.

May we heal beyond a core wound.

Breathing More Deeply More Often

Are we breathing or being breathed?

Are we taking quick, shallow breaths, or are we deeply filling our diaphragms?

How would our life change if we breathed more deeply more often?

Might we become more present?

Might we become more peaceful?

Might we find increased mental clarity?

Might we have additional energy?

Might we sleep better?

Breathing deeply used to give me a stabbing pain in my chest.

Now I have the gift of breathing deeply, which brings me into the moment, sharpens focus and reminds me that I'm a human being with the gift of life to smile, to share and to grow.

On the way from pain to deep breaths, I offer my body more attention; I receive chiropractic care, a series of Rolfing treatments, regular massage and craniosacral treatments.

Now I move more than before via brisk walking, hula hooping and weekly Pilates. I experiment with Bikram (HOT) Yoga. How interesting to invite my body to breathe and move in ways it hasn't since I was a pony-tailed tomboy playing outside until dark.

To you, dear soul, and all the deep breathing you live into.

Chapter C

Cages to Recognize and Unlock

What images arise when you think of the word ***cages?***

Take time to journal if you'd like.
Zoos.
Bird cages.
Gates.
Bars across windows.

What about our hearts?
Have you considered the cage of your heart?
What does this phrase mean to you?
Are your feelings constricted?
Do you feel strongly? Do you follow your feelings? Would you say you follow your heart?

What needs to shift for you to listen to the whispers of your heart?

What steps might you take to open your heart?

In a journaling class on the topic of Wild, I stun myself during a silent exercise when I realize how much I live with white gloves on, in between such a small boundary, how much Wildness is missing from my choices.

No one but me is holding the key to the locked cages of my youth, edicts such as *you should, be quiet, you better not do that…*

What a revelation to my psyche…could it be time to allow something in me to act with more abandon? To color outside the lines?

Does this strike a chord in you?

Are you wearing the metaphorical white gloves of childhood, trying to be a good person when it's time to stretch beyond old mores to live into your wild, authentic, joyful self?

The next week, I twirl before my *Course in Miracles* sisters, announcing, "I am going to take up space."

Pushed away a lot as a girl, told to be quiet and to go somewhere else, I am the sister in the Rambler's back seat, straddling the hump in the floor. I am the one tucked into cobwebby corners of the basement without discovery during rainy day games of hide and seek.

In my 40s, something within me isn't used to taking up space.

At all.

Until a Monday morning when I'm ready to twirl in front of friends, claiming a measure of a new way to be.

This newness leads me to a poetry class, to clean out a closet full of overly large clothes and to be seen, at least a little, realizing that maybe it isn't necessary to hide any longer.

Consider a cage to unlock.

Outside the Lines

My steady husband's baffled
"Are you the one I know?
You're acting rather odd these days
Such changing to and fro

You're looser 'round the edges
You cross against the light
Causing me to wonder who
Slips next to me at night

Your recycling's less than perfect
And you smile more and more
Are you the one I married?
Or has she scooted out the door?"

The answer's elementary
I'm Joy and doing fine
I've just reached a new decision
To live outside the lines

I've tiptoed over time and love
Never noticed it before
Life feels sweeter from this place
May I live here evermore.

Calisthenics for the Contents of Our Craniums

I don't know about you, but as a little girl, I wonder how to feel peaceful when the world presents war, famine, kidnapping and more. I don't understand how to feel settled while chaos swirls.

Later, I don't feel I can be joyful if someone I know is faced with a challenge. How can I be happy when my classmate is in the hospital? How can I feel peaceful when Dad yells because Mom forgot to put today's mail on the table?

As an adult studying *A Course in Miracles*, I encounter radically diverse ideas.

I could see peace instead of this. *A Course in Miracles, Lesson 34.*

Oh my!

Really?

How do we train our minds to do this?

It is from your peace of mind that a peaceful perception of the world arises... *A Course in Miracles*, page 51.

By shifting our minds from anxiety or worry, for instance? Yes, by believing the Holy Spirit instead of the whining, comparing, complaining voices of our egos.

Let's repeat these thoughts another way.

We can shift our minds where the ego wants to keep us wounded and small to believe in the glory of each moment, and the beauty of who we are.

A rich book that can help lead us there is called *A Course in Miracles.*

You may be aware of the *Course* through Marianne Williamson's best-selling book *A Return to Love*, which offers reflections on *Course* principles, or through another avenue.

Have you studied the Course?

Might you join a group soon?

Would you consider starting one?

Do you have curiosity to check the book out of the library?

Years before entering a *Miracles* circle, I hear about the gathering, suspect it could be a cult and believe it isn't anything I'm ready to try.

Raised in a Reform Jewish household and a recent convert to Christianity, I'm not feeling open to another mystery until I say *Yes* to a friend's invitation; Sally will pick me up Monday.

Whoosh!

Despite the book's language that takes patience to understand, it doesn't take long to become hooked as a regular attendee.

Where else can I gather on a cold morning in a

warm home where tea leaves steep and coffee brews, while the scent of fresh cinnamon cake wafts near?

Where else can I sit with engaged folks interested in healing into better versions of themselves?

Where else can I receive hugs from women and the occasional man supporting one another with questions about ego, conflicts with friends and more? How much better could a week begin than joining a loving circle?

I gain friendships.

I grow in spiritual wisdom.

I smooth rough edges of my ego.

When a *Miracles* Sister shares that she practices kindness with herself, the idea rattles in my mind on the drive home, and again throughout the afternoon.

Kindness with myself?

Are you kidding?

Perfectionist me?

Could I possibly treat myself with any of the kindness I extend to others?

What a wild idea.

Maybe I could give it a try.

And I do.

One small step at a time, I treat myself with slivers of kindness, despite the harsh internal critic who runs my life.

Try a little kindness toward your sweet self.

Callings from the Deep

What do you think of when you consider the word ***call****?*

Have you heard calls inside that lead you down a particular path?

To me, it means a knowing and/or an intuitive understanding of directions to follow.

Typically, we're more aware of our five senses—sight, taste, smell, touch and hearing—than of our six mental faculties named in a program called *Prosperity Plus,* by Mary Morrissey. Mary asks us to awaken to our Imagination, Intuition, Memory, Reason, Will and Perception as we expand into fuller expressions of our lives.

Here are three examples of calls on my path:

1) In August 2007, I receive a knowing to become a spiritual director. A month later, we move from Ohio to the mountains of western North Carolina, and within a week, I receive an email from Emilie, an Ohio friend, with the link to a spiritual direction training program.

Looking up *The Haden Institute*, I'm in awe, because I hadn't told Emilie about the call I'd received, and because the program's site gives me goose bumps, mirroring my interests and nature, plus it's practically around the corner.

Due to filled classes, trips to Ohio and our marriage unraveling, I enter a class in April 2009, graduating in January 2011.

Halfway through, I heal enough into myself to birth an idea I'd received upon waking years earlier, an idea knocking on my soul, birth me, birth me. Journaling to understand the dreamy images, I discern beautiful fabric around the neck with positive messages into the world, an idea that becomes locally sewn wares of Batik cotton blessing people and spaces through *Joy on Your Shoulders* (J.O.Y.S.)

2) I receive a knowing to become a Hospice Volunteer and shortly thereafter, I enter training, which is beautiful and comprehensive.

I suspect, too, that all I learn may come into play with my parents, dear ones aging who live a couple hours away.

Indeed.

The following April, Dad calls before dawn, "Joy, come be with Mom; I called 911. I'm in congestive heart failure."

Yikes! Please, please don't die before I get there, Dad, my heart pleads.

Thank you to the Heavens and back that I can pack for an unknown amount of time to drive safely to Charlotte, North Carolina, and that Dad lives longer. Belted into the passenger seat? A deepened sense of presence and supporting grace.

3) I receive a knowing in December 2014 to write the first edition of this book, along with the title and structure.

Thank you, thank you.

This call with a way to approach it resonates with my creative passion, desire and reason to write this book—to inspire all of us to live into increasing aspects of our peaceful, joyful selves.

Respond to a call to heighten your joy.

A Chakra Ready to Clear

Historically, I have been a mouse. Or a girl in a woman's body. An insignificant person in the room. My voice hasn't been heard.

No one will respond when I say something astounding. Next, another person will say the same thing to cheers.

Do you know what I mean?
Do you or someone you know lack voice?

That was me—no personal power, no voice, until one day years ago when Ben's on the computer at my house.

I stand nearby naming ideas to inspire joy through my work. When I say one goal with more doubt and ego than the others, an intense pain strikes my throat.

Screaming as an intuitive response to clear it, Ben says, "Joy, why don't you go into the laundry room so the neighbors don't think I'm hurting you."

You've got to love Zen-like Ben who doesn't freak or tell me to stop yelling; he states a relevant comment with all the calm he possesses. This totally is a guy you want by your side in a crisis, as well as on the way to a procedure like your first (and last) colonoscopy.

In the laundry room with the door closed, I scream, then chant OM, clearing and clearing my throat chakra.

Exiting, I collapse into Ben, who has risen from the desk. He holds me as I cry with joy, rambling about this surprising occurrence which feels golden, that I'm meant to have voice for JOY, and how great that my throat chakra has cleared.

To all the power and voice we can have.

Does Change Have Our Number?

Does the word ***change*** *make us shrink back?*
Smile with delight?
Break into goose bumps?

My responses to the word definitely have changed over time. Maybe yours have too. And who knows? Maybe soon, you'll have a change of heart about the idea.

After all, acorns become Oak Trees. Seeds become Sunflowers. Babies become Toddlers...

My latest understanding regards the ever-expanding Universe and our abilities to expand into fuller, freer ways of being. Whatever we can imagine, we can live into!

I'm having a blast imagining *Go In Joy! An Alphabetical Adventure* as a best seller, allowing us to meet on tour…hooray! I'll read a few sections, answer questions and sign your copy.

Years ago, however, I am reluctant to change due to the lack of control I felt as a child and the illusion of control I felt I had in life.

Along comes my husband, ready to stir things up.

Ready for a new kitchen, he's the guy who works it all out. He's the one researching a new computer, the visionary set to buy land in the mountains and the Dad on fire to add a puppy to our lives.

While Wally bubbles with ideas, I am healing through layers of emotional wounds from childhood, balancing the needs of family and writing poetry.

I go along. I adjust. I walk our puppy, Spice, wondering if we'll *really* build a mountain home in the future and move to North Carolina.

Time flows on.

Friends who've relocated say it takes two years to adjust to a new place, so I figure I'll prepare ahead. I'm not interested in languishing on a mountaintop with grief to work through.

The year before we head south, I plan to work through my feelings leaving everything I'm used to—my friends, my church home and our house, the one holding seventeen years of memories.

Right.

Tears.

Walking Spice.

Tears.

Packing.

When it's too snowy and cold to emerge much in February, I hear that this year the spring journaling class I love holds a synchronistic title—*Letters to the Future.*

Oh my…could this be more perfect?

Responding to Jenny's provocative prompts, my understanding grows from a reluctant woman leaving all I love and know in northeastern Ohio to an excited woman living into the future, certain that God will surround me with support. I also receive a knowing that my healing has stalled in Ohio, and new healing will enter.

The change to Brevard, North Carolina is beyond wonderful!

We wake to shifting cloud views through floor-to-ceiling windows in our radiant home. We sink into the hot tub on the screened-in porch before supper. I smile entering the master bath of iridescent granite that features a soaking tub surrounded by happy ferns.

New friends invite me to soulful groups that resonate with my being.

We begin the tale of this big change in our lives.

Let's welcome change!

Consider a Dose of Courage

What does the word **courage** *bring up in us?*
What have we done that takes courage?
Do we practice it with regularity?
Why or why not?
What will change if we take courageous action?

One day our older son rallies his brother to vacate the playroom by making three piles: *give away, basement and bedrooms.* Before the last action figure retreats, I plant my stake. I've long been ready to crouch beneath the basement stairs to claim a soul-centered spot. Thanks guys!

Shopping for a writing chair for this new space, I announce I'm growing out my gray hair to a saleswoman, who tells me I'm brave. Returning home, I write an essay that my decision isn't brave compared to firefighters, war heroes or others on the front lines of life and death. I suspect this is about conformity, individuality and the beauty we pursue and/or allow to shine through.

Ultimately, I return to coloring, though those days are numbered. In the summer of 2017, I receive a knowing that it's time to fully embrace my natural, whole Self.

I imagine that many of us deal with a similar decision, stepping into arenas where acceptance, beauty, perception and identity swirl in myriad ways.

I see, too, that certain choices I've made have taken courage, the kind that starts in our hearts before speaking in the world.

This has been a journey moving through fearful

thoughts, taking one courageous step at a time, leading to increasingly courageous decisions.

Following my heart to become a Hospice Volunteer brings me through training into hospital rooms with patients in their last days, and serves my parents when they desire support.

Following my heart to post on-line leads me to create a website and a regular newsletter for subscribers.

Following my broken heart to enter a friendship with Ben leads to a beautiful relationship followed by living together.

Sharing with Ben that we may not belong together any longer, I discover he's felt it too.

It takes courage to leave relationships, to reach out to friends who've pulled away and to experiment in life.

It takes courage to make a decision to be healthier and to take steps towards that goal.

Courage connects our hearts with living more fully.

It takes courage to tend our interior gardens, to grow ourselves into stronger, more peaceful, more joyful beings.

It takes courage to surrender to our destiny, to connect daily with our Higher Power and to live more deeply into love.

Call on courage, dear one.

Creating Every Day

Author, speaker, activist and awesome creator Jan Phillips has a CD series called *Creating Every Day—Making a Masterpiece of Your Life, a step-by-step Guide to Conscious Creativity,* which I love.

I've listened to it at least three times, plus writing this reminds me to begin again.

Jan's series is filled with inspiring stories of the gifts of creativity, and her website—www.janphillips.com—overflows with visionary books, CDs, cards and more.

Recent Sunday afternoons, Michael and I sit in the living room where he massages my toes and feet as I read aloud from an amazing book of Jan's that's long graced my home, Divining the Body: RECLAIM THE HOLINESS OF YOUR PHYSICAL SELF.

"...The spirit within seeks expression in the world without, and we are its voice, its instrument. In the very heart of our own matter is the one that calls out to be heard, the love that yearns to be shared. This is our life force, our vitality, transcending boundaries, merging inner and outer, human and divine, thought and matter in an endless cycle. It is through our feelings and senses that we perceive this force, and through our feelings and senses that we share it with others. In our creative works, this force gets carried from soul to soul, heart to heart. We pass on God in the gift of our creations..."

Creating Every Day.

Our Creator fashioned this world, allowing us to express unlimited gifts of creativity.

We can knit, dance, paint, color, build bowls with clay…

We can create and create.

Or can we?

Do we have a big judge inside telling us we can't?

Do we stop ourselves before we start?

Do we spend time on activities we could pass on, so we're unable to pick up a pastel?

Are we spending too much time on Facebook? Pinterest? Lamenting lost love?

What can we release to free ourselves, so we can play more often in life's open fields of possibility?

What if we give ourselves thirty minutes, a table, a drawing pad and a box of crayons?

What if we give ourselves fifteen minutes, a notebook and a pen?

What habit can we tweak in our week to open a space for creative play?

Believe me when I tell you how blocked my creative flow was years ago, and that unblocking is **totally** worth the journey. I'm in awe that I'm seriously writing a second edition of my first book *Go In Joy! An Alphabetical Adventure,* after other books have come through to bless readers.

Here's a peek into how I was creatively wounded:

Dad yells, "Why would I want to go to the band concert? Those kids can't play!"

Indeed.

And off we'd go with zero parents in tow.

Today, I respond for my youthful self to Dad's rhetorical question boomed years ago—

Well Dad, you attend to silently cheer us on as we do our best, though we're not Grammy-winning musicians or scheduled for Carnegie Hall. You attend by setting aside your pipe, newspaper and evening at home.

Yes…the seeds of my creativity were unintentionally planted sideways, leading me to grow weeds until I'm led to a seminal book on creative recovery, *The Artist's Way: A Spiritual Path to Higher Creativity* by Julia Cameron, a book I work through three times, until I kill enough Kudzu to write an essay or two and to attend a poetry circle, planting a tulip border to the creative garden I'm evolving into.

Gremlins occasionally chime in…*Who will read it? Remember that guy in college who said you write drivel?*

Gremlins, Gremlins. Thank you for sharing.

I'm writing a bestselling book called *Go In Joy! An Alphabetical Adventure,* and I look forward to meeting you at a book signing.

Create any day; begin today.

aMUSE Me

Leave lipstick on my collar
a red rose in your hair
sway your hips this way, Babe
It's time for an affair

Come close as spirit moves you
sweep me off my feet
on the page we'll dance till dawn
a sultry, Latin beat

I'll feel your words surround me
your adverbs teasing in
pronouns brushing past my cheek
creative mode near sin

Description down my slender arms
your touch across my hand
pulsing ever faster
to the red-hot Salsa band

We'll be the last to leave the floor
you'll lead me up the stair
laying down words to consummate
our musing love affair

Play the Part of a Poet

Live between dream lightning, rise at dawn.
Write until your fingers tingle, notice
green promises out your window.
Let a vacation bloom in your heart.
Write waterfalls, add children dancing.

Listen when chocolate whispers, *Lick the knife.*
Serve spaghetti without silverware. Slam
active verbs to the mat. Wear a zucchini hat
to breakfast. Watch an ant trim
his handlebar mustache in the mirror.

Sit quietly. Press your ear to white wicker.
Rock to Bora Bora. Sip bug juice. Count
mosquito bites. Scratch a lottery ticket.
Give a mixed bouquet to a stranger.
Blast Springsteen. Meditate. Wear

Purple socks. Make Popsicles in Dixie cups.
List words that rhyme with bliss.
Make a fist. Kiss your knuckles.
Pray for peace. Write a love poem
to a blue hydrangea.

Walk with open eyes, an empty mind.
Breathe all of life in.

Unexpected Shower—3:30 a.m.

Parched cells call out as if stranded
in the desert with a hollow canteen.
All of me wants to keep still, dissolve
into cotton sheets' womb.

Slipping to dim-lit kitchen, I slice
an orange, let juice spray my throat
to imagined applause. Follow
with an encore, half grapefruit.

I slide into my writing chair, follow pen
across blue lines from here to where?
Unwind bucket, pull up enough words
to wash over all of me.

Crossing a Bridge of Belief

Have you heard the tale about the newlywed who cuts off the end of a ham before baking it?

When her husband asks why, she says because her Mother always did. When her Mother comes for dinner, they ask her why, and she replies that her Mother always did.

A call to Grandma reveals the reason: Her roasting pan was too small to prepare ham without cutting off the end.

I've recently heard more than once that beliefs simply are a collection of thoughts that repeat in our minds.

Beliefs simply are a collection of thoughts that repeat in our minds.

Beliefs!

How many limiting or false ones do we tote around?

Can we offer a bit of willingness to reconsider a belief or two?

Does the word chiropractic bring up ideas within us?

Are we comfortable with alternative modalities, with traditional medicine or with a blend?

Do we experiment with practitioners on the advice of friends?

Do we believe in our body's natural abilities to heal?

The 1960s…

Because Dad is an internist with strong beliefs, and because there is wide understanding against the practice, we hear over and over that chiropractic is akin to swearing.

2005.

Women gather in a cozy home on Lake Lucerne in Bainbridge, Ohio to study *A Course in Miracles.*

My friend Emilie says, "Joy, look how much straighter I'm standing today. I'm thrilled! I'll give you the name of my chiropractor and massage therapist in case you're interested; they're great."

In case I'm interested.

Emilie's words strike a highly-interested, sweet spot in me, albeit wary, because nine years earlier my car was rear-ended and totaled. Ever since, though I've tried everything my doctor recommends, my friend knows I'm challenged by chronic neck and back discomfort.

Chiropractic care is suspect, of course, since my neural grooves repeat Dad's mantra against the practice, echoing his ***deeply ingrained belief.***

But my friend's invitation sparks a question in my heart—*If my car was totaled, could it be that my frame was damaged, as well?*

Journaling the next morning with our Beagle curled against my slippers, I write and pray about crossing this bridge of belief.

In a couple days, I call for an appointment, trusting that Emilie's referral is a sign to follow.

Completing paperwork in the waiting area, I am nervous, wondering if I belong here.

In the treatment room, Dr. Randy swiftly understands my history and concerns, putting me at ease. He explains a plan to guide my recovery from the accident.

And we begin.

When the therapist my friend loves works on my neck, I marvel as I feel facets of the accident leave my body.

Ahh…

My frame becomes more comfortable, giving me confidence to thrive.

Cross a bridge of belief.

Chapter D

Daily Practices Feed Our Beings

Do we start days in a rush with the news on, crunched to get others and ourselves ready to leave the house?

Might we wake early, breathing into understandings that align with soul…that all is well?

Do we run from dawn to dusk, falling asleep in front of a television program?

What can you change, so that your days open with space to take deep breaths?

Years into my divorced life, I'm on a road trip with Dan. Come along!

Crossing the parking lot after our late lunch, Dan asks me to take the wheel into Ohio.

Approaching the car, I'm startled to see broken glass

on the ground. Then I look up. "The passenger window's gone!"

"It's a Smash and Grab!" Dan replies. "They took my backpack!"

Oh, my.

A flood of feelings and emotions lands inside me.

After a moment, I find my way to a nearby curb where I'm able to sit down, reclaiming center, breathing into gratitude.

I'm grateful that Dan and I are safe and that my car wasn't stolen. I'm grateful that my conference inventory is intact. I'm grateful the window can be replaced.

Later, sections in books bring the incident into focus, reminding me that events are neutral; it is we who bring unique perspectives to all that happens.

Yes.

I moved through trauma into a calm place, because I've long breathed into stillness, sinking within to connect, filling scads of journals, including gratitude journals.

A gratitude practice allowed me to shift from victimhood to thanksgiving.

May you lean into practices that fortify your center, enabling you to breathe through what life offers.

Let's live in ways that support our days.

Let's Touch on Death

I wonder whether it's wise to include this topic in a book inspiring joyful living, and I decide it is.

If you're currently grieving the loss of a loved one, friend or pet, you have my deepest compassion. I understand, and I'm truly sorry for your loss.

This may not be the time for you to read this essay or the two poems that follow… consider skipping ahead to page 69.

My journey losing loved ones has been painful, beautiful and tender. I've learned plenty about saying little while breathing into all the actions of my heart…being as filled with love as possible...hugging longer, holding hands with tenderness and bringing plenty of tissues.

One of the most comforting books I've read about death is *Home With God in a Life That Never Ends* by Neale Donald Walsch. I cherish this book, and I often recommend it.

Learning to accept the idea of dying allows us to more deeply love our lives. I believe that beyond fearing death, life calls us to embrace it with more gusto than ever.

Life invites us to suck popsicles to the stick, lick honey from palms and sip hot cocoa before marshmallows melt. Life asks us to say what we mean, jump up and down and laugh as joy overflows our hearts.

Life asks us to celebrate sunrise, praise raindrops and kiss roses swaying in the breeze.

Smile to the clouds, hug trees
and skip to the mailbox.

May we live into juicier lives.

Missing You, Grandma Ruth

Could I struggle into white tights,
buckle black patent leather shoes,
peer into the reflection of you?

I see you conducting dinner with mom,
chopping chicken livers in your corner kitchen,
shooing me away to find something to do.

Marveling at your soot-covered windowsills,
I wonder how sleep will find me—
horns honking, ambulances screaming,
discordant notes down Brooklyn's neon streets.

I try your Jack LaLanne exercise bands,
finger ivory on your baby grand,
begin my geography homework.

Now tears fall for childhood memories
that sing in my head without your story,
that sit
without your warm lap
beneath them.

Shell-shocked

Your son flies home today from the front lines
where hospital linoleum reflects a legion of fears—
battle weary
from seeing death as close as your blue eyes,
worn out
from the cancerous wave of news that ravaged his reserves.

I wait,
my thin-stemmed emotions seeking balance
like crystal wine glasses on a mantle's edge.
From five states away,
I see your shrinking silhouette
tucked into crisp white sheets.

Dinner and the News

Families.

Traditions.

Odd patterns.

Our beloved parents, doing the best they can or could.

Considering families, what traditions come to our hearts?

What traditions do we celebrate and replicate?

Are we holding pain from something that happened years ago in our family?

May we find our path to forgiving the past.

I've released layers upon layers of this nightly family tradition:

Mom calls us to dinner.

We step over the pet gate to sit in our turquoise swivel chairs pulled up to the round Formica table.

"Joy, it's time to turn on the news," Dad says.

Hopping over the gate to scoot into the living room, I turn on the Huntley-Brinkley Report to its nuclear noise level before dashing back, hurdling the kitchen barrier and returning to my seat, sweeping despicable peas beneath the meat.

Every night at our house, the routine plays like a record album on repeat.

Dinner and the news, joined forever, as my soul cries in silence at the lack of connection.

How can we be yelled at when we ask for the ketchup to be passed?
How can no one ask us about our day?
Why must we eat dinner WITH the news?

So many times I leave the table to cry in my room, releasing distress I feel with this pattern we're required to keep.

As an adult, I play it over in my heart. I write essays and poems. I eventually release it as a family quirk in a family of wounded souls who don't understand much about intimacy.

Connect as richly as possible.

Family History

At the end of the street,
a flock of Canada geese
gathers every day. They
float on the lake, wander
into the road, block cars
as we exit the neighborhood.
Today, one lone goose
honks from the spot,
Where have you gone?
I'm here alone!
He's the lost child
in a grocery aisle—
he's grandma
demanding attention
when I am small.
Nana pays us
a dollar to write her
a letter.
I hunch over the task
with a gaggle of spinning
thoughts hanging near.
My father hates his own
mother, this Nana who
whines from Wisconsin.

When Dad was eight,
she threw his birthday watch
against a wall,
shattering it
along with something
inside my father that
rages the rest of his life.

Collared

A company in France manufactures
citronella anti-bark collars for canines,
expensive, but worth every quiet moment,
and not considered a cruel correction.

As I read poetry in my sacred room,
our young Beagle surveys the street scene,
spies the neighborhood greyhound trot by, barks once,
receives a snoutful of spray from his collar.

Puppy pads over from his lookout spot
bringing a citrus-like freshness along,
rests silken ears on slippered feet,
shifts into a Norman Rockwell scene.

I imagine a comparable collar for Homo sapiens
available in designer hues and jeweled,
which sprays when we utter a negative word,
changing us into a simpatico species.

Dreams to Reel In

What dream have we been holding?

What dream can we reel in?

What longing weighs on our hearts?

Can we take a step towards it?

What discontent or longing scratches the edges of our thoughts?

Reel in a dream is an early *Joy on Your Shoulders* saying, and it's a keeper.

I'm all about it.

For years, I journal the dream on my heart...to be the Joy I am created to be. I know I'm not her with this heavy sack of perfectionism and other wounds from childhood. I'm hiding in clothes too large. I'm comfortable being invisible. I feel like an outsider in groups.

My dream is to heal into the Joy my soul came here to be...the peaceful, joyful person I believe I can be.

Hooray!

I first feel like a semblance of her in 2011.

Have you heard that if we take a confident step in the direction of our dreams, all manner of Providence steps in to support us?

Here's a tale of the heavens moving:

Ready to birth the first *Joy on Your Shoulders* (J.O.Y.S.) creations with positive messages, I decide to hire a seamstress. Opening the newspaper, I jump back with astonishment when I see *JOY'S Specialty Sewing Service.*

If this isn't Providence moving in my direction, I don't know what is.

And this wonderful seamstress named Joy, who turns my long-held idea into joyful wares that bless souls near and far, hardly ever advertises…of course.

Take steps toward your dreams.

Of Dreams

Rain drenches a yard,
rivers run banks
chasing lives to higher ground,
and you do a rain dance
in your mind, gaze
upon cracked mounds of earth,
dream of water sprites.

Some dreams before yours and mine
died in silence, some spent time
behind bars, some took flight.

Awake or sleeping, we choose a path.

Wake up, my friend.
Come dream with me.

Chapter E

The Surprising Gift of Energy Healing

Are you familiar with energy healing?
Have you experienced gifts of this practice?
Is this the first you're hearing of it?

I first experience energy healing in the spring of 1997 when I ask my friend Emilie if she has ideas to relieve my aching back after a car accident. She suggests I contact Marilyn, a soul we know from *A Course in Miracles.* Though I'm not sure what her practice is, I implicitly trust my friends.

Marilyn guides me into a candle-lit room where soft music plays, telling me to remove my top and pants and to lie on my back beneath the sheets while she steps out.

Returning, she gives me a rose quartz crystal to hold on my belly and prays in a quiet, inviting tone, invoking unseen entities to draw near.

Before long, I see in my mind's eye myself as a sad, wounded child with parents unable to give me what I need. Next, I see my parents as sad, wounded children with parents unable to give them what they need.

When I witness the entire lineage on both sides to the beginning of time not receiving what they deeply long for, I feel to my core immeasurable forgiveness, compassion and love for my ancestors. Energy streams from my fingers in an intense and lengthy way I'll forever recall, along with knowing that generations of negative emotions stored in my body are exiting, offering me an extraordinary gift.

After that surprising event, a new relationship arises with my parents. I'm able to breathe beyond their antics without judgment, and my stomach no longer hurts when we're together.

Living closer to Mom and Dad years later, I visit often while honoring myself: I pack earplugs for the loud news programs they love, bring food I prefer and fold workout clothes into my bag for daily walks. We have better visits than ever, while I receive a bonus…the chance to stop at Trader Joe's on my way home.

Peace within and without on visits to my parents.

Priceless.

Visit an Energy Healer to support your healing.

What Experiment Beckons? Go Forth!

Does the word ***experiment*** *take you back to Science class?*

Me too.

Besides science experiments, I see the word in a fresh manner, as in experimenting with newness in our lives.

Do we venture towards the unknown?

Do we shrink back from newness in our lives?

I haven't always tested the waters of experimentation.

Some years, I am stuck, perhaps slightly depressed, reading old newspapers and magazines, not taking much initiative. This version of me carries wounds and low self-worth which make it challenging to move ahead.

Perhaps you resemble me at that unproductive stage, or you experiment. If you're hiding from life, may you uncover the source of your distress, discovering ways to heal and blossom into smiles and joy, our birthright.

My run with experimentation begins in earnest a decade ago when I ask Elise whether or not I should attend a gathering for entrepreneurs. New in business, I wonder if I qualify, and my friend says, "And why wouldn't you go?"

She knows I'm a fan of the presenter, the program is being held nearby and I can afford it.

Indeed, why wouldn't I go?

Because voices in my mind shout that everyone will be more advanced in business than me, that I don't belong and that I won't know how to dress, etc.?

Yes, because voices in my mind are noisy.

Quieting these passengers on the bus of my ego, I advance, inviting Elise to join me for our first event of this nature, which turns into a fabulous experience.

An attendee I talk with one evening is so excited about my creations with positive messages that she tells a store manager down the hall she needs to carry them.

The manager says *Yes,* giving me my first wholesale order.

That fall, I say *Yes* much more than ever, understanding that each new place I visit translates into opportunities. I meet folks who buy wares, I network, or I learn to cross a mismatched group off my list.

Experimenting feels like following energy…living into new aspects of myself…engaging more deeply with life.

Experimenting opens us to new opportunities and new relationships.

Experimenting leads to new hobbies.

Experimenting allows us to discern which activities work for us.

Experimenting rocks!

Add experimentation to your life.

Chapter F

Fizzies and Other Childhood Treasures

Read the following question before daydreaming about your life as a child.

What did you love to do?

Here's some of my daydream: Root Beer Fizzies. Twinkies. Rolos. Bazooka Bubble Gum. Beatles Cards. Roller Skates. Chinese Jumprope. Hours of jacks. Marbles. Freeze tag. Red Rover. Mousetrap. Monopoly. Careers in a red box, imprinting on my heart that Happiness points are better than Fame points. Dancing around the living room singing *Dites Moi* from South Pacific. Hula hoops. Pogo sticks. Throwing balls over the house. Climbing crabapple trees. Coasting bikes down

Trumbull Hill. *Heart and Soul* on the piano. Playing school.

Trading with girlfriends.

After games of kickball, tag and jacks, one of us yells, "Let's Trade!" We scatter home to search junk drawers, treasure boxes and more to come up with stuff—plain or wrapped in tissue and tape. A whistle, a rabbit's foot, a Beatles card, a marble, a piece of Double Mint. We run to the meeting spot at the set time where the fastest draw goes first, offering an item for auction. We place bids forward.

"I'll give you this barrette and this lanyard for your rabbit's foot."

On and on the trading goes until someone's had enough.

Trading isn't something I'll likely resurrect, but hula hooping sure is, which earns an essay in Chapter H, a second reminder to resurrect an element of childhood.

You have permission.

And, yes…I know where my jacks are…call to play!

Add an element of play to your life!

Mom, Do You Remember?

I see snapdragons and petunias today,
climb memory to the top of a flowering
crab in our backyard to watch us planting
together when I am nine. You teach me
to dig a suitable hole as I squirm
at the sight of worms passing through.

I'm wearing my favorite pedal pushers
and red Keds with white laces
in the years of freeze tag, hours of jacks,
jumping up the drive on my pogo stick.
We take a zillion trips to get warts
frozen off, you slather lotion on the
ringworm around my neck, say I stink

When tomboy me avoids the tub.
And our trips to the grocery store—
I am your Pop Bottle-Returner,
your Total Adder-Upper,
your Cart Runner-Backer. What a team.
How often we hiccup our way home
after eating fresh rye in the car.

Forgiveness Frees Our Hearts

What's our experience holding onto blame or regrets, which can become more entrenched as resentments?

Are we, or do we know someone holding onto a resentment eons after a dispute with a spouse, parent, or sibling?

How is that serving us?

Have we allowed disturbing feelings to move through, so our hearts are open to love?

When we've lived in our mountain home for a year, my husband shares news it's time for our marriage to end.

As Wally names reasons, a voice inside me says, "*Take in this darkness. You need it. You're going to transmute it.*"

How interesting.

My soulful self knows I need to absorb this shock instead of pushing it away, which I'd much rather do, since the scene arrives as cognitive dissonance; *this can't be happening!*

Me?

A divorcee?

Our family breaking apart?

I do the best I can, grieving this loss to my core through tears, fitful nights and baths, before oversharing my wound with anyone near. Yes, I need to hear myself repeat what happened to help me believe it really did.

Eventually, I repeat the story less, praying that forgiveness will enter my grieving heart.

Months later, I gratefully receive forgiveness in a hands-on healing service when Ben and I visit Lily Dale, a Spiritualist Community in New York, releasing me from anger that feels entrenched.

Hallelujah!

To all the forgiveness we can receive, allowing us to live more joyfully.

Five years after divorce, my former husband invites us up the mountain to share Thanksgiving with him and his wife, our grown sons and other family. Ben passes, I'm honored and the day is fun, comfortable and a gift to my soul, reuniting with a few relatives I haven't seen in years.

My ego notices changes in the house and the view that's no longer mine, to which my integrated self smiles.

I drive home with leftovers for Ben, along with my overjoyed heart that Wally and I are this amicable, healed and comfortable whenever we meet, particularly this Thanksgiving.

May we find our way to forgiveness.

Freedom from a Mind of Fear

I humbly admit that I love my life these days.

Smiling more often than not, I reach for my gratitude journal and devotionals most mornings. Folks sensitive to energy tell me I offer a sweet presence.

Gratitude. Love. Peace. Joy.

This newer way of being in the world feels like an amazing gift, an eternal gift available to each one of us when we've crossed an interior bridge of understanding.

Maybe we were raised by parents who were wounded by their parents, people who didn't know how to meet our needs, soothe our fears or love themselves.

We may have adopted habits that don't serve us well, like overeating, too much sitting or compulsive shopping.

We may be holding onto too much stress, too many responsibilities or too many items in our closets.

We may have tried to fill our lives in ways that felt right, yet ways that added separation from ourselves, our families or our understanding of our connection to the Cosmos.

We've left behind, healed through, released and otherwise vacated dreary corners of our minds where fearful thoughts abide. We've left abusive husbands, betraying wives, alcohol abuse, perfectionism, anger…

We've come to the Light. We've surrendered to the Deity of our understanding.

Or have we?

Where do we find ourselves?

While I've been guided through decades of healing edges to cross this bridge, I'm not sure I can provide a trusty map.

Walk down various avenues, some mentioned in this book. Try balance, kindness, gratitude. Seek a spiritual mentor. Watch less television. Forgive yourself. Sit quietly to connect with all you cannot see.

Lean into Love within and without while quieting the fearful, protective, untrue voices of ego, voices telling us not to trust inner knowing or that we're not enough.

We need to sink into our soulful selves, the ones in concert with our Higher Selves, the ones who always know exactly what we need to do.

Lean into all the Love you can hold.

What Life Teaches

1

We are unrepeatable miracles
Who could have been ants, plants

Or otters playing in a river.

As spiritual beings in human form,
We agreed to bring Heaven to Earth,

Though we may have forgotten.

Families, friends and teachers
Can hurt us so much that we

Tuck inside or rage out of control.

2

When we desire to live otherwise
Beyond fears and beliefs in mind,

Limiting thoughts, ego distractions

We read books, attend conferences,
Remove distractions, seek silence

To evolve into a new kind of human

Who embraces our wondrous,
Out of balance world

With Love.

Chapter G

Friends as Invaluable Gems

Do we treasure our friends?
Do they know how much they mean to us?
Do we long to connect more often with a friend?
Can we reach out today?

Friendship. Do we remember good friends, as well as rocky days of shifting alliances?

I recall playing jacks on the cool front porch, sleepovers between purple sheets in a purple bedroom and cotton candy at carnivals.

High School friends we meet for pizza, muddy fields we march down and awards we accept on stage.

In college, friendship seems truer, colorful secrets

swirl like a kaleidoscope and how many friends still abide in the center of our hearts? Love to you, Ellie! Marie and Kelly, I'm so glad we've reconnected!With marriage and children, friends arrive and retreat. Remember Euchre, Trivial Pursuit and stroller walks up neighborhood hills?

In my sixth decade…friendship feels continually new, old and just right.

How we support one another, hold one another and celebrate together.

How I love connecting with girlfriends on the phone, in person and through Zoom during the Covid-19 pandemic.

How I love visiting guy friends, though maybe there's just Randy, who rocks on the West Coast. Writing this reminds me to reach out more often.

Hey Mary! Dear Emilie! Linda!!! Elise, dear one! Barbara Jean, Emily, Kara and Catherine!

Perhaps nothing feeds our hearts as much as a soulful conversation with one of our friends. Heaven knows how much we treasure topics that exist only between us, the way we get one another, the ways we uplift each other.

To all the friendships we nurture, appreciate and celebrate.

Connect today with a friend.

Gift Exchange

You name the Kingfisher for me.
We watch him ring the dinner bell
from our riverbank perch.
Walking on, you hand me nature
wrapped in eight shades of spring's lustrous green
ribbon-tied with purple flowers.

I name your burdens pressing in.
We sit on decaying tree fall
connecting in quiet.
In one suspended moment, you hand me your heart
wrapped in tumbling out layers of pain
which I untie to hold with care.

Girlfriends

At ten, we play
a Heart and Soul duet
on the spinet in your den.
Samantha twitches her nose
in a black and white flicker
on the Magnavox behind us,
while on the couch
Uncle Marty with the bulbous schnoz
spits cherry pits into a bowl.

Feldman Brothers Produce:
your family's fridge overflows,
carnival of fruit
dancing over the shelves
like a merry-go-round cut loose,
and around the dinner table—
running chatter, interruption,
clatter of hands rustling
for seconds, thirds,

the noisy jockeying of family,
a fountain of grapes, plums,
peaches flowing
onto the table,

out into the night,
rainbow ride home
that feeds me
heart and soul,
though I don't know it's so.

How Much Gratitude Do We Express?

Do our backgrounds and/or current lives include complaints, critique and whining about the state of people and situations?

How does this affect the way we act and feel?

Would we enjoy smiling more, seeing increasing beauty and allowing life to unfold, instead?

In my childhood home it's taken decades to deeply forgive, airtime plays a rowdy list of criticism, perfectionism and negativity, with fun, love and zest for life mixed in.

My family's ways cause me emotional pain, shame and wounds I carry on my back in a rather heavy sack, until I'm able to release them. Layers heal in divinely perfect ways, starting with Morning Pages, a practice Julia Cameron presents in *The Artist's Way: A Spiritual Path to Higher Creativity*.

Writing three longhand pages upon waking to empty the contents of our minds and hearts means our early pages will hold anything and everything, from complaints to grocery lists, from reminders to ourselves to lines of poetry.

And how long can we complain in writing about a person or issue in our lives without doing something?

This moves us to speak to another, to begin exercising or to join a group, right?

Of course, I can't speak for you, but I, for one, am a person who can't write long about an issue before I'm compelled to seek a solution.

These days, my heart rides a pretty straight lane between what's bothering me and taking action. If it's bugging me, I'm going to talk about it, write a letter or tweak the way I'm living, most days; other days, I'll sleep on it.

If writing down a complaint inspires you to take action, that's great.

Maybe you even turned a wider corner as I did; my morning writing now begins with a Gratitude Journal. Then, in my daily journal, I offer thanksgiving for all that transpired yesterday and for the blessings today will bring.

Since re-starting my Gratitude Journal in 2011, life reveals a new rhythm which holds more joy, more appreciation and more allowing with how life unfolds.

Practice gratitude to uplift the rhythm of your days.

Who Knew? Grounding Matters

Are we new to the idea of ***grounding?***

Do we feel like we live in our heads or that we're unsteady when we're alone?

Do we stand barefoot on the grass to ground as a regular practice?

It's a beautiful day in Cleveland, Ohio, May 1, 1996. Our sons are at school, my husband is out of town and I have an appointment to interview a woman named Faith at our sister church in Cleveland's inner city.

Entering the highway, I hear, *"Don't go."*

Because I'm not grounded in my body, plus I've never heard the idea of grounding, I figure this voice is fear in my mind, reflecting hesitation to drive where I've never gone.

I don't interpret this message as wisdom from my Higher Self, intuition or a message from Spirit Guides, as I would now. Today, I would turn around, cancel the appointment and dream up an option for the newsletter.

In 1996, however, I hold legions of perfectionistic tendencies—I have an appointment, I'm on deadline and a voice I interpret as fear isn't going to keep me from my plans.

Praying for protection, I drive on.

Close to our sister church, my brain registers a look of horror on the faces of those in the car stopped at the red light to my right…SLAM!

My car is rear-ended with a jolt, sending me through the green light, my seat breaks and my head and knee ache. When I'm finally able to stop my car at the curb on this one-way street, neighbors descend to check on me.

At the hospital, I'm diagnosed with whiplash, soft tissue neck and back injuries and a mild concussion; my car is totaled. The man who slammed into my vehicle suffered a seizure with his foot stuck on the gas.

Years later in the mountains of western North Carolina, I connect with a group studying Bill Plotkin's book, *Soulcraft, Crossing into the Mysteries of Nature and Psyche,* and I'm led to heal into a grounded person. This newer way of being leads to deeper breathing, mindfulness and allowing, along with the ability to honor voices of warning or guidance.

Look into becoming grounded to expand your joy.

Chapter H

Healing One Area Can Shift So Much

Truly.

What could we intend to heal, take steps to release and live into that will improve our lives?

If we treat ourselves with kindness, what might arise?

If we stop focusing on someone else's life and pay attention to our path, what will change?

We can forgive someone from our past.

We can stop worrying about the future.

We can move more. Eat less. Drink more water.

We can list reasons for gratitude instead of complaining.

We can treat ourselves with kindness.

We can clear a pile of papers.

We can give away clothes.

We can turn off the television.

We can stop playing an internet game.

We can spend less time on Facebook.

We can call a friend.

We can take a walk.

We can light a candle, say a prayer.

We can take a bath.

We can write a letter.

We can stretch.

We can read a spiritual book, a poetry book or anything.

We can sit on a sunny bench listening to birds.

We can hug a tree.

We can imagine the love of all life coming into our beings.

We can give hugs.

We can transform an old belief into a new understanding.

Healing one area of our lives will energize our joy.

Our Beings Are Becoming...

...their true selves
to bless us and all we meet
on this road traveled less —
the one mystics dance along
saying yes more often to signs,
hidden messages in bark,
lines on a page, and sharing tea
with angels unbidden on the road.

This opening into newness
on the edges of our future
calls more and more
like birds on the dawn,
telling us to rise, inviting us into
a new kind of siren song,
healing once and for all
any doubt we carry still.

What Are We Hiding and Why?

Did we ever hide something, and then forget where we put it?

Have we tucked secrets into our pockets for some reason?

Are we hiding in clothes too large for our frames?

Are we hiding something about ourselves we're afraid to reveal?

Are we hiding our light?

Consider the idea of hiding, and take a pen and paper to journal if you'd like.

I suspect as children we may have gotten used to hiding certain things.

As adults, are we still hiding items or issues from others? How honest are we?

What if we name our truth?

What if we live in ways that deeply honor our heart's desire?

In our marriage that ends, I hide parts of myself, responding to a request by my husband not to display my spiritual nature. I make peace, instead of living authentically, because that's what I understand about relationships at the time.

When my relationship with Ben is new, I tell him I'll be honest. I no longer will keep parts of myself hidden, and I understand that for our relationship to thrive, openness is the best medicine.

This dear man has so allowed me to be who I am on any given day, and I am grateful. With his love, I've shed my invisibility cloak, stretched into new ways of sharing my understandings and gifts and healed into love for myself, which allows me to share love with others, including you, beloved reader.

In the fall of 2014, I feel larger energies enter, telling me I no longer belong in relationship with Ben, calling me to experience higher aspects of life. When I bring it up over dinner, Ben says he's felt it, too, that we're no longer resonating as partners. The next day, he offers to move to the lower level of our house, so I don't have to move out.

On March 3, 2015 at a potluck gathering of the spiritual center I attend, Dan attends as a guest, where he hears me say I'm Joy, inspiring peace and joy through my being, wares and a book I'm writing called *Go In Joy! An Alphabetical Adventure.*

Dan lights up, because he had received a message to *Find Joy in His Life*, along with the knowing he'd recognize me…and he does.

Ben, Dan and I share this house in ways that work amazingly well, until a shift enters.

When my relationship with Michael is new, he tells me how easy I am to be with, because I'm honest and direct.

Live beyond hiding with increasing honesty.

Beyond Hiding

Tucked no longer
Into worry, judgment, fear
And a host of self-conscious feelings
That made walking in front of others
Painful.

Tightly wound no longer
With shoulders to ears
And a host of physical maladies
That made life in general rather
Painful.

Living above the neck no longer
Ignoring intuition, gut feelings or
Guidance from angels
Which made our willful lives
Painful.

We smile with ease and laugh
From time to time.

For we live in trust, freedom
And the joy that comes from
Opening our hearts, loving what arises
Supported by all that makes days
Blissful.

Are you Highly Sensitive, Too?

Do loud sounds bother you?
Bright lights and fluorescent lights?
Temperature extremes?
Are you highly sensitive in other ways?

When I discover Elaine Aron's book, *The Highly Sensitive Person, How to Thrive When the World Overwhelms You,* I feel understood for the first time in years, learning I'm wired differently than many people. Her words inspire me to offer myself a measure of grace. Yes, I need more rest. Yes, I easily become overstimulated.

Easing up lays the groundwork to release other layers of perfectionism.

Fast forward twenty-five years. I venture with wariness and curiosity into my first Bikram (HOT) Yoga class. While I've long been a person to avoid excessive heat and intense exercise, something attracts me to this experience.

Oh my. This is the sweatiest, longest workout I've tried, and I continue to return, for it feels like an enormous gift to my being...from my heart to my lungs, from my flexibility or lack of it, to challenging my strength and balance.

During my sixth visit, an intriguing awareness arises—that I've long identified as a Highly Sensitive Person (HSP) who avoids loud sounds, temperature extremes and chaotic vibrations. I have a history of running away from uncomfortable circumstances.

Is my nervous system more challenged in Bikram? Am I resting more often because of it, or because I'm a beginner staying in the room? How interesting…I'm not running away. I'm hanging in there. I'm managing.

Cooling down after class, tears begin to fall. My instructor pats my back, saying kind words about this breakthrough, about sensitivity and power.

Honor your nature, and challenge it, too.

Honoring Each Person We Encounter

What does the term ***honoring*** *bring up in us?*

Have we felt honored?

Do we honor others with ease, or do we judge and reject?

I'm pretty sure honoring one another isn't a typical style many of us have grown up with, but likely more of a learned practice.

So much depends on how we're feeling about ourselves. For example, if our parents didn't love and care for themselves, they may not have honored us. When we, in turn, don't love and care for ourselves, we're challenged to honor others.

But as we heal into deeper levels of loving ourselves, we cherish, nurture and honor our beings, enabling us to share these attributes with each person we encounter.

Becoming better and higher versions of our magnificent selves, we extend blessings and honor outward.

Begin by noticing your preferences; then honor them one at a time. Notice how you treat yourself. Notice if you belittle yourself. Begin treating yourself with a layer of kindness. Live into increased moments of honoring yourself.

Before long, you'll have enough honor to share.

How much honor can we live into and pass along?

Surprise…Hula Hoops!

Do we long to break out our jump rope or pogo stick?

Do we ache to paint with our fingers?

How much creative play can we add to our day if we bring back an element of childhood?

Studying Julia Cameron's book *The Artist's Way: A Spiritual Path to Higher Creativity,* I'm encouraged to write down three things I liked to do as a little girl. One of them is hula hooping.

The next day, a pink, plastic hoop greets me out of place in the frozen food section of a discount store, a message I receive with a smile. The hoop hitches a ride home, inviting me to sway to a rhythm in my cells.

Hooping in a circle of women on retreat as I tell a story, one friend says, "You should make a video for YouTube!"

Maybe so, though at the time, I'm cruising dark alleys in my invisibility cloak.

Years later, Wild Women clap and holler as I read poems while hooping. Afterward, I reflect—*that was wild! I read serious, soulful poems while gyrating—what an oxymoron, which worked. It was fun, and my audience loved it.*

These days, I hoop in the living room after long stretches writing, or under a sunbeam on the lawn.

Bringing play back into our lives invites creative dreams to return, spirits to lighten and smiles to broaden.

We're as young at heart as we'd like to be.

Run to the corner. Do a puzzle. Shoot a hoop.

What childhood activity can you engage with today?

Chapter I

I Am—Meaning that Matters

How are we doing and feeling?

Do we find life traveling in directions we like, or do we wonder why things aren't better?

Could it be that our language needs an upgrade?

When we say things like, "I am sick, I am never going to get ahead or I'm not able to afford new clothes," we call these events into being.

We're that powerful, and I suspect we can use language without realizing how it affects us.

Phrases arise with ease *"I'm so tired…I'm short on time. I'm never going to lose this weight."* We say these kinds of things all the time, especially if we're not awake to what we're saying.

Consciously noticing the words we say and think truly matters.

Making positive I am statements creates an altogether different outcome.

Here's a snapshot from my Gratitude Journal, 4.29.20

I am grateful for Spring beauty everywhere.
I am grateful that Michael's such a dear man.
I am grateful that my books inspire readers.

Practicing positive language leads to unlimited blessings.

What we put out reflects back to us!

Make positive I Am statements.

Allowing Inspiration to Open Us

Have we ignored the touch of inspiration in our lives?

Have we tiptoed onto the path of an idea?

Are we living into the gifts of an inspired life?

When you consider engaging in an inspired life, how would you live?

I didn't intend to follow a message of inspiration into all that's opening for me, but hindsight shows Divine Orchestration at work, which I believe ALWAYS occurs.

Divinity LOVES us into more of our soulful selves with our willingness to grow, with intention in our hearts.

Where can we allow more growth into the fullness of who we are?

Follow whispers of inspiration we receive. Engage with them. Draw them. Dance them. See where they lead. Enter their echo beyond boxes we inhabit, higher than all we hide behind.

Follow seeds of ideas into the playroom, into discovery, into transformation within and without.

Uncover gems shining into new facets of our own becoming.

Become more of our radiant Selves.

My journey from isolated, scared and safe in a small

world of fantasy to a peaceful soul sharing joyful wares grows my sense of risk-taking, confidence and passion.

Woo hoo!

I've grown from a timid woman who received an idea to an awakening woman whose energy speaks before I say a word.

Crazy.

Perfect.

Here's where the seed is planted...

At a writing conference at Punderson Lake Park, a woman exuberantly praises Jan Phillips and her book, *Marry Your Muse.*

I buy the book, highlight with vigor and soon hear that Jan Phillips will present a Creativity Workshop in the Cleveland, Ohio area, where I live.

Attending, I am wowed and highly inspired.

What an amazing workshop!

Waking, I receive a cloud-shrouded idea, so I slip into my writing chair to follow my pen, seeking illumination through journaling, until the idea gels.

I call fabric artists and meet with folks who sew, though I don't seem to get very far. Movement is tentative, guided by an internal thermostat which registers low esteem.

Years later, I buy fabric, visit a screen printer and contract with a seamstress, intent on giving radiant creations to a circle of friends who will celebrate my 50th birthday and our move to North Carolina.

These first Batik creations say *Notice green promises out your window* and *Make a fist, kiss your knuckles, pray for peace,* lines from the poem *Play the Part of a Poet,* which appears on page 56.

Wally and I move to the mountains of western North Carolina where I feel called to become a spiritual director. Our marriage ends, I move out, then move again. In addition to studying spiritual direction at The Haden Institute and dating Ben, I join a community leadership class where I meet a man who invites me to join a Mastermind Group.

My consciousness grows through the Haden program and Masterminding, healing me into new aspects of myself, enabling me to re-birth the creations with sayings like *Cultivate kindness, When chocolate whispers answer* and *Reel in a dream.*

Turn to the essay called *Joyful Wares to Share* on page 229 for the evolving tale.

Follow ideas to expand who you are!

Trusting the Wisdom of Our Intuition

Do we honor whispers of intuition?

Are we blocked from receiving intuitive messages by voices in our heads?

Can we see in hindsight when our intuition was right on?

What treasures of partnership or periods of separation with intuition are yours?

Personally, I can feel like a beginner listening to mine, even though we've spent glorious time aligned. I imagine this feeling lingers because of the intuitive hit I miss when my car is totaled. This tale is relayed in an essay on Grounding in Chapter G.

Admittedly, my intuition leads me to open my broken heart to Ben after my marriage ends, to become a vendor of joyful wares at larger venues beyond my comfort level and to give Bikram (HOT) Yoga a try, though I've long avoided becoming overheated or intense workouts.

Each of these entries into new aspects of loving, serving and working out widens life in amazing ways beyond an initial move forward.

Step by new step, our lives expand and expand.

Grounded and centered in healthy ways, we receive messages from intuition.

These intuitive sparks lead us deeper into living fully and joyfully.

Thank you, intuition…you rock.

Honor intuition to power possibility.

J

Chapter J

Jessica Chilton

If you are writing a book, who rises to the top when you consider who matters to you?

If you're not writing a book, who matters to you?

Let these people know how much they mean to you with a phone call, a letter or a gift.

On my journey saying *Yes* more than ever, I meet Jessica Chilton, a shining soul who shakes me up in wondrous ways.

After working with Jessica, I write a testimonial for her website, which is featured for a time, and which follows this paragraph. Jessica has continued to evolve, expand her offerings and incredibly impact so many. Her current site is https://www.jessicachiltonspark.com/

"Before my Creative Wellness Program, there was a big gap between who I wanted to be in the world and how I was choosing to live. With Jessica's amazing guidance, I moved through internal blocks to a more integrated peace within, stepping fully into who I really am, finding my footsteps on the right path. I now love my whole self and am living into my destined work to inspire joy through my business, *Joy on Your Shoulders!* I am grateful for the confidence, self-love, purpose and passion that shine through me and my business daily."

Jessica's support tops any list my heart writes whose presence and work positively influenced me.

Specifically, Jessica introduces me to the idea of forging a truce with my inner critics, enabling me to sail forth. First, I tell Jessica how often I swear at them, banishing them to dark corners, leading Jessica to offer a fresh perspective.

She asks me to name the inner critics speaking within. I name my Inner Banker, Inner Time Keeper and Inner Sloth among the unwelcome guests.

When I later share this exercise on the phone with a friend, she names her Inner Slave Driver and her Inner Diva.

Next, Jessica asks me to write down the benefits of each voice, allowing me to see the positive ways they serve. Lastly, she invites me to converse in my journal with my Critics, Myself and my Higher Self.

I write, "Inner Critics, why are you so noisy?"

"We took over, since you weren't in charge of your life," they reply.

"Oh my! Thank you so much for all you've done. That's great! But we're in charge now," Myself and Higher Self say in tandem. "What if you stay on in supportive ways as we work together?"

Ever since, we're in tune, lined up, acting in ways that best honor me, others and the ways I can be of service in the world.

How joyful!

Make a truce with your Inner Critics.

John Fox

Are you familiar with poetry therapy?

Are you ready to release emotional pain you haven't yet expressed?

Attending a poetry writing group, I learn that a John Fox Poetry Workshop in Lakeside, Ohio is open for registration.

Hooray!

Lakeside is where we marched during Band Camp. When I hear the town's name, my memory skips down that lane of whistles and drills, plus fractured sleep in an overheated barracks of a dorm.

Additionally, I've heard great things about John Fox, author of *Finding What You Didn't Lose.*

I drum up the courage to ask my husband if he'll stay with our sons for the weekend, enabling me to attend. Though I'm unaware, requesting this weekend away is a start…to begin listening to myself beyond roles as a wife, mom and volunteer, and for Wally to develop a closer relationship with our sons.

Over the years, I enter a couple therapists' offices seeking answers for an overflowing bucket of emotions I haven't expressed, though too many tears fall as I attempt to respond to questions. Instead, I run from their couches, playing out an entrenched pattern to retreat from discomfort.

In my first John Fox circle, I come home to myself among others deeply feeling, expressing and breathing into the sacred space John facilitates.

I recall the singular souls gathered, red tulips waving and words rising to clear stagnant blocks of fermenting pain.

Dear ones who gathered in that sacred circle, bless you, bless you. I hope you're doing well these days.

John Fox has since written *Poetic Medicine*, led many hundreds of workshops and more. He founded the Institute of Poetic Medicine, which funds poetry-as-healer projects throughout the United States. Its mission is to "awaken soulfulness in the human voice." https://www.poeticmedicine.org/

Enjoy a poem I wrote at my first John Fox workshop plus two poems by John, a peek into the depths of this soul I'm honored to know.

Give a John Fox workshop a try.

Letter to My Workshop Leader

Excuse my late arrival.
I know you requested
we come back at nine o'clock.
But my walk after breakfast
engraved an invitation,
sang its morning song to me.
Truly, sir,
I never meant to linger
only mosey up the lane
and return by nine again.
How could I?
Squirrel chattered all excited
in his oak across the way
as swooping right before me
flittered screeching, intense jay.
I understood you warned us
to be seated right on time,
but as I walked on further
a soft breeze caressed my cheek.
Red-Winged Blackbird in a tree
introduced himself to me,
"O-ka-lee! O-ka-lee!" and
I'd never seen one before
or heard rainbow's end in song.

Vibrant red bands accented
the polished glow of black wings.
I paused to know his story
and how he feels in spring.

When Someone Deeply Listens To You

When someone deeply listens to you
it is like holding out a dented cup
you've had since childhood
and watching it fill up with
cold, fresh water.
When it balances on top of the brim,
you are understood.
When it overflows and touches your skin,
you are loved.
When someone deeply listens to you
the room where you stay
starts a new life
and the place where you wrote
your first poem
begins to glow in your mind's eye.
It is as if gold has been discovered!
When someone deeply listens to you
your bare feet are on the earth
and a beloved land that seemed distant
is now at home within you.
— John Fox

Poetry

She skates boldly onto
the page, tips one vulnerable foot
back and forth slowly, till finally
the edge of a toe
cuts a simple, sharp line
through the world's cold resistance
and with that plain courage,
a statement of intention begins;
and you can't turn back any longer
from the weight of feeling and letting go
into the flow that follows.
Poetry is a choice to feel it all,
not all at once but gradually to sink down
within ourselves, to give what fear
we hold behind our knees
to gravity and grace,
to discover what makes
our whole world turn;
the place our necessary weight
lifts to lightened joy.
— John Fox

Journaling as a Spiritual Practice

Do we journal in the morning? In the afternoon? In the evening?

Is it something we might try?

Part of my morning devotional time includes prayer journaling, a practice that delights me, precedes my best days and serves as a place for my Higher Self to guide my ways. On these pages, I give thanks for yesterday and thanksgiving for the day unfolding.

In Ohio, my morning writing transforms over time. At first, I empty my mind of stress and lists, along with worries about family. Later, a friend enters my conscious awareness, I write a prayer honoring her and later that day, our paths cross—magical, since we haven't seen one another in ages. Ahh…it's beautiful to feel so connected.

In North Carolina, synchronicities seem less tied to what comes through my pen. Mornings reaching into myself connecting with all we don't see grounds me, centers me and aligns me with the highest good I'm guided to live into.

Days breezing into activity without settling into this practice, I later feel scattered, like something is amiss until a whisper reminds me what I overlooked, calling me to sit, to breathe and to write in my sacred chair.

Returning after days away is returning home. Guides are near, my breathing slows and I am held in the womb of Love.

Thank you, thank you.

May we give our souls space and time to express hidden understandings on the page.

Give journaling a chance.

Sleep Writing

If I write, if I shuffle straight from sleep
to my sacred room and close the door,
don't worry that I'm staying away from you.
It's just that morning thoughts are difficult
to capture—they disappear in an instant
like bubbles blown through brittle wands
or late spring snow meandering down.
I write upon waking to pick words
fresh from their nocturnal vine
and to commune with heaven
between the lines.

Julie Andrews

Has this actress brought you joy, too?

Imagine little girl me wearing my favorite pedal pushers as I run to sniff the lilac bush...dreamily floating along with song because of *The Sound of Music* and *Mary Poppins,* starring Julie Andrews.

These movies make my heart sing, my smile wide and my joy palpable.

I'm in heaven singing these tunes, dancing around the yard and fingering the piano keys in the cool basement most days before dinner as a way to curb my desire to eat NOW.

Her roles live in me, no matter how much or little I watch these movies.

I appreciate you and the characters you've brought us, Julie Andrews.

Thank you!

Chapter K

What if We Kick a Habit?

If we kick a habit, what will enter?

If we stop complaining about what's not working in our lives, will we start to be grateful for what works?

If we stop racing out the door in the morning, will we begin an evening routine which sets us up for an easy exit post toast?

If we'd like to stop eating when we're not hungry, will we reach for our water bottles between meals, waiting until we feel sensations of hunger?

I believe in waking up, being conscious and noticing what's not working in life. Then I like to shift something to alter results.

Here are a couple small examples.

I notice that the terry liner in my shower cap often is wet, and I'm tired of putting the wet cap on my head.

Ah ha! I can buy additional caps, rotate them and wear one with a dry liner. Simple. Just right.

When our Beagle, Spice, nearly pulls me down a mountainside, my upper arm is sliced by his retractable leash. Dressing years later, my left shoulder consistently aches.

I vehemently ask out loud, "When will I put my left arm in first?"

This irritated-with-myself question awakens me to don jackets, sweaters and coats leading with my left arm, a new habit to replace longstanding discomfort...nice.

Look around, dear reader.

Tweak a habit to improve your outlook.

Chapter L

Leaning into Leftovers

How do we feel about leftovers?
Are we creative in the kitchen or rigid?
Do we store lots of food or shop often?

Sharing an apartment with a girlfriend in 1979, my visiting flame can't believe how little food I store, or that my mate hijacked the freezer. He reacts in a flash, covering a record album with foil to deliver fifty percent of the freezer to me, which gives me concurrent feelings of horror and humor.

I can't believe we're doing this!

Yep. There it sits: one silver barrier with her food crammed into the left side of the freezer while the right side holds something like two hot dogs and four ice cubes.

After divorce, I may enjoy the best meal ever. The next few days, I disregard it, because I've lost interest for the same thing. It feels odd to write this, since I've traveled far to the opposing camp.

Now it's normal for me to enjoy leftovers, without a microwave. After reading two articles in quick succession against the appliance, I give it up, since they echo my musing…*is it really a good idea to heat food this way?*

Winter afternoons, we make a large pot of soup or chili for easy/breezy dinner days two, three and four.

Then there's this practice from the former queen of rigid ways—mixing leftovers to reduce items in the fridge while creating impossible flavors to replicate, like quinoa and rice added to leftover lentil soup, combined with leftover tofu cooked with onions and turmeric…sensational, and likely a singular happening.

You do this as well? Great! Isn't it wonderful to lean into leftovers?

To all the leftovers we can savor.

Let There Be Peace on Earth

Has this song affected us?
Have we longed to be peaceful?
Have we discovered peace inside?

As an earnest, skinny second grader, I sing *Let There Be Peace on Earth* with every fiber in my being, understanding that for peace to come on earth, each one of us needs to heal into our own.

When girlfriends ask buck-toothed me to agree with one side or another, I can't. I see each perspective making sense—that each one holds her point of view.

Growing up, I have a repeating dream I'll write something that will add peace in the world.

I skedaddle into spaces of serenity when Dad's anger erupts.

As an adult, I more deeply understand the lyrics, knowing them to be true.

Let there be peace on Earth, and let it begin with me.

For there to be peace on Earth, each person must heal into peace.

For there to be peace on Earth, I will heal into peace.

In my journal, I pray to live into a peaceful person.

I begin by limiting the amount of news I breathe into. For twelve years, I haven't had a television, opening my time and heart into more of a reader, more of a writer and more of a person breathing peace in and through.

And who knows?

Maybe this book fulfills one little girl's repeating childhood dream.

Take steps to become peaceful.

For Naomi

(After a talk given by Poet Naomi Shihab Nye)

You stand small in stature,
tall inside my heart, the way
you speak peace from humble lips,
the way you walk in poetry,
read it in the hall to wake your son,
tell science teachers,

"Write a poem on the chalkboard,
not to dissect it or explain it,
but place it there as a witness
or just because."

You give me courage to stay
on this path of poets before me,
to speak the truth I see
that others rush past, to keep
my fragile dreams for peace
alive.

Let It Begin With Me

(for Tim)

Peace
Peace
Peace

Please

Pleading

Perhaps

Perchance

Per country

Per day

Per hour

Per minute

Per person

Perfection

Peace

Listening as a Sacred Art

Listen.

What do we hear?

Are our minds quiet?

When another speaks, are we forming our answer, or listening with our hearts open?

Do we talk more than we'd like?

Is it time to listen in a fresh manner?

When Ben speaks early in our relationship, I show him I'm intently listening by nodding my head and making sounds like "um hum" until he guides me to be silent and still while listening.

When we share a home, Ben places branches near the bird feeder for those who perch, and sets a steel bowl into the earth as an avian bathhouse. His understanding of birds, gardening skills and endless practices with nature arise from years of deep listening. Whether listening to me, meditating or sitting on the deck in a lowering sunbeam after work, Ben displays listening grace.

How my life is enriched living with this man who listens well, while influencing the evolution of my listening practices.

In 2011, I enter a period to connect with all we cannot see, honoring a call to spend time listening to my soul, which seeks sacred union. I write about my experience in an essay titled, *What Separation is Ours to Heal?* in Chapter S.

Years beyond living with Ben, I date Michael, who displays aspects of deep listening with reflective comments, letting me truly feel heard.

May we listen differently than before, uniting with the wisdom of the ages between each breath.

Let's listen like beginners.

What Longings Are Ours to Unravel?

What do we long to be, do or have?
Can we advance toward our longings?
Can we release a longing that's fantasy?

When the instructor asks us to write what we long for, I know—I've lived for decades with this longing that my older sister pay attention to me. Naming this leads me to write a poem about us and to reach out to her.

Big Sis apologizes, saying she didn't mean to hurt me…that it's just how she is…she can ignore everyone who lives out of town, managing all she can handle in view.

Whew.

Reaching out lifts a huge psychological weight, freeing me to send her gifts, cards and anything I'd like without being attached to the outcome.

Releasing this longing opens me to release additional burdens…like sitting in church longing for my husband to sit beside me or wishing my mother had been present.

I begin to see life beyond fantasies and longings in my mind, a discovery that guides me to the present, where life happens.

Years later, when the facilitator asks us to write who we want to be, what we'd like to do and what we'd like to have, I run to the microphone, bubbling over with a life of transition.

"I love everything about my current situation, and I'm in deep gratitude. There's nothing else I want to be, do, or have. Maybe I don't really have a question. I just don't think I can do this exercise. Could that be? Does this make sense?"

These days, I long to deepen into the Joy I am created to be. I long to share love, peace and joy on the road, honoring my Self more than before, wherever I am.

I am beyond grateful that I'm no longer compacted, scared and hiding.

What would you like to Be, Do, or Have?

Chapter M, N

Mark Nepo

Have you met Mark?

Have you encountered the writings of this poet, philosopher and bestselling author who's been on a path of spiritual inquiry for more than thirty-five years?

Years before I buy *The Book of Awakening: Having the Life You Want by Being Present to the Life You Have,* a friend of mine repeatedly brings up his name.

Mark Nepo. Mark Nepo.

Elma is in love with Mark Nepo.

When I finally discover his writings, I, too, fall in love.

Thank you, thank you, Mark Nepo.

Your beautiful prose illuminating our souls' understandings and your vulnerable sharing of what it means to live an authentic life touch inmost places in our journeys to heal, to be present and to shine our lights.

Touched by your inspired words, we are blessed.

I love any of Mark Nepo's books I've read, for each holds treasures, and I'm grateful that Michael and I attended one of his talks in Asheville, North Carolina in 2019.

Thank you for your courage, your voice and your presence in our lives through all you write, teach and share.

Thank you for living into so many radiant aspects of your soulful self, Mark Nepo.

Treat yourself to a reading of Mark Nepo.

A Message Arrives in Stereo

Have you heard a voice when you're home alone, knowing it hasn't come from a person?

In April 2016 as I apply blush after a quick shower, I hear a voice in the air above and behind my right shoulder.

"How can you reach more people?"

Flustered due to a time-crunch-feeling rising inside, I manage to say, "Thank you. I can't think about this right now; I need to get to class."

Traveling the four-lane road for a journaling circle, I muse with gratitude about other messages I've received from Spirit.

The day my mother-in-law Sarah dies, I discover her favorite cheese in the fridge with that day's expiration date…when my husband ends our marriage with words that land in my gut like a black cloud, I hear, "Take in this darkness. You need it. You're going to transmute it."

Next, a strong thought arises to stop musing, to be present on the drive.

Surprising myself, I arrive early, before both students. These moments allow me to prepare the table and to sit with my eyes closed, breathing into stillness.

When Diane arrives, sitting next to me, she's more serious than I've witnessed.

"Joy, I don't think you understand how valuable

the questions you ask are. I am growing and changing because of this class...you need to put them in a book!"

Struck by inspiration, my hand rises to hold my heart, challenging me to speak right away.

When I share beyond the awe I feel, I let these two know that Diane's given me a meaningful answer to the question I'd earlier received.

Wow.

The next two weeks overflow with events and commitments.

Anytime I'm home, though, I allow powerful, playful journaling prompts to arrive through my heart and hands, adding up to a book that reaches more people.

Go In Joy! Venture to Your Center—Journaling Prompts to Enliven Your Joy is the second book Divinity writes through me to bless readers.

It makes my heart smile that this book of meaning filled questions with space to write supports those ready to understand themselves in new ways.

May we receive messages that guide us onward.

Chapter O

A Recipe for Lovers of Olives

Enjoy this recipe encouraging us to eat healthy fats before a meal; it's appreciated every time I bring it to a gathering.

Savory Olive Tapenade

1 teaspoon capers*

¾ cup pitted green olives, chopped

¾ cup pitted black olives, chopped

2 cloves garlic, minced

¼ cup olive oil

1 teaspoon lemon juice

2 tablespoons fresh basil, chopped or dried, to taste

pepper, to taste

**Ever since running out of capers, I leave them out, happier with the outcome.*

I prepare this with olives nearly as pure as they grow, without additives. I often add cut-up artichoke hearts, which we love. In the past, I added tofu or couscous. Experiment!

Combine all ingredients in a bowl.

Important note: Hand cut the olives or use a food processor, but your mixture with a processor will resemble moist cat food, which you may not prefer.

Serve with baked whole-wheat pita or your favorite crackers.

Makes 10 servings.

Serving size: 2 tablespoons of tapenade. Calories per serving: 74.

Saturated fat per serving: 1 gram.

Recipe from www.realage.com

Chapter P

What if a Pandemic Arises?

Do our cupboards hold a good supply of staples?

Have we saved money for an emergency?

Are we settled inside our souls, or do our egos lead with fear?

How ready are we to stay home for weeks?

In the United States and many countries of the world, March 2020 (or earlier) finds us living other than freely gathering, flying off to Tahiti or meeting friends at our favorite restaurant.

We're warned to stay home, while much has stopped running the way our planet and days used to run.

We practice social distancing.

We may know people who've contracted Covid-19 or who've lost their lives to this virus or another.

We might wear masks or gloves when venturing out.

We may order essentials online.

How are we doing in our minds?
Are we losing sleep, fretful or frightened?
Are we peaceful, hopeful and optimistic?

A plethora of news reports and anecdotes abound.

I'm grateful that the long road I've been on to become a peaceful person beyond an anxious ego serves me and others these unusual days.

Mostly, this time lands inside me with calm, breath and ease, allowing me to uplift those who connect.

I believe in the best humanity can be.

May this reset raise the consciousness on our planet, so that we become kinder, more compassionate and more loving to one another.

May we live through these unique times with grace.

Releasing Layers of Perfection

How has perfection influenced us or not?
Can we make mistakes without beating ourselves up?
Do we let others make mistakes without blaming them?

When I hear we're Perfect aspects of Divinity, I agree; at the soul level, this absolutely is true. As we heal, our soulful, authentic selves are divinely Perfect—loving, joyful, peaceful, compassionate, generous…

However, the perfectionism Mom carries and passes along to us is a different animal. It is a fear-based need to look or act put together, a mask that all is in order with huge concern for what others will think.

It is me feeling my outfit looks wonderful, and Mom pointing out the scuff on my shoe. It is me cleaning and cooking to exhaustion before guests arrive. It is me adding stress over newsletter fonts with the church secretary. It is me believing that if certain things happen, I won't be able to forgive myself.

Perfectionism creeps into tasks like grocery shopping, laundry and decorating. It makes life unmanageable, preventing spontaneity, ease and laughter.

Blessings on our upbringings with perfection and critical comments from family that make us feel our efforts aren't good enough. Bless all the wounds we receive that we need to heal so that we can be kind to ourselves and compassionate to those we meet.

I deeply understand we're each a Divine Spark of our Creator, that you are in me, I'm in you and that many of us carry heavy wounds, some we don't even know we carry.

How interesting that we're led to heal in our own time and that we can heal into greater versions of ourselves, shining ever brighter.

I suspect some of us heal very little during this lifetime, which is just right, and others receive tremendous healing.

Release the need to make everything perfect.

Our Journeys Ask Us to Persevere

Do we abandon our goals or see them through?
Can we stay the course until our journey is complete?
What shift in perception do we need to trust our process?

Moving through discomfort during colon hydrotherapy, a.k.a. colon cleansing or colonics, my therapist congratulates me for staying with the process, returning over time.

Korey says clients sometimes abandon the journey of cleansing or any journey too soon, and we agree that goals require us to hang in there. She and her teammates know this beyond any doubt, for they raced across the United States after training on and off bikes for years.

Eva, my Pilates instructor, comments on the long path my body and psyche have traveled to become open and flexible, naming my ability to trust the process.

Wow.

I hadn't thought much about it. Admittedly, the path has been a lengthy, complex one to unlock my rigid body and understanding from contraction, fear and suffering into comfort, ease and allowing.

It's not that I consciously trusted the process, though. I think I followed an innate desire to release tightness and constriction in my frame and mind, somehow able to stay the course.

Progress happens!

Take writing a book, for instance.

We may hold an idea for years. We may know exactly what book we're meant to pen, yet something holds us back from starting.

When we move through the issues that block us, we could find ourselves taking action every day, producing a completed book, if we stay with the journey.

An image from one of SARK's colorful books jumps into memory. I believe the section guides readers through procrastination/overwhelm cleaning a closet. She writes something like, "The first day, open the door, removing two pairs of shoes. The second day, extract three shirts," instructing readers to take baby steps.

Yes.

Everything large is accomplished by taking one small action at a time.

One day at a time.

Life's journeys evolve, dear one.

Name a goal.

Stride into the journey, and stick with it, persevering until the end.

Journeys are worth the effort to complete them.

Chapter Q

Seek a Quiet Mind, Grasshopper

Are we intimate with this idea?

Might we enjoy doing a little less to be a bit more?

Might we enjoy driving with the radio off or with our iPod unplugged?

When's the last time we were home without sound on in the background?

Have we given meditation a try?

Is it time to begin again?

Early in relationship with Ben, he sits on my backyard deck to be, watching the light change, observing squirrels chase branch to branch, catching a whiff of steak from the neighbor's grill.

I join him, but only for a moment, while my brain spins with all I need to do, and before I hop up to address a task.

Or, I sit longer, bouncing my leg up and down, until Ben asks if I can stop, likely meaning, *Can you resist adding nervous energy to our shared space?*

Experimenting in my unfurnished rental, I begin living without television, which opens time, allowing me to dance with life's bountiful offerings and silence.

Plus, my stress abates by unplugging from televised news or regularly reading current events.

Later, Ben crafts a meditation bench for me, an invitation to begin this way of being and breathing.

My inconsistent sessions continue to this day.

Though I regularly don't sit long, Being and Silence easily have my name in ways they didn't long ago. I gain peace by sitting to journal, pray and breathe, and I have the gift of a relatively silent house.

Expand time welcoming being and silence.

Elephant Rock Reminisces

My heart races as I remember,
though it's worth the quickening to continue.

It is just the other day, say fifty years ago or so.
I hunker in the sun warming my shoulders,
sashay with the breeze, grooving to Robin's song
when a beautiful girl races to me, climbs aboard.

Imagine!

She tests the contours of my shoulders, neck,
spine, to find a comfortable seat, locates the exact
spot I'd polished for such a happenstance.

The young woman arrives heavy with sorrow,
and her long locks cast a shadow on my brow.
I feel the weight of her heartache, hold what I can.

She comes another sunny day, and another.
She brings pen and paper, writes poems
to soothe rough patches in her teen life.

The young woman begins to skip to me,
her heart lighter, her smile more radiant.
We bask in the sun's glow together,
enjoying a bond I'll call Love.

She loves me, and I love her.
Our times together are intimate, joyous,
never long enough for my longing.

Though I know she'll grow up and move on,
I don't think it.

And then it happens.
One day she wears a wedding dress.
Another day she drives away.

I hunker in the sun warming my shoulders,
sashay with the breeze, dream of the song we shared.

Chapter R

Releasing Frees Us Up

What are we holding onto?
What's ours to let go of?
If we release a long-held pattern, what will emerge?

When I let go of mailings from Publisher's Clearing House, I don't realize what will unfold.

When I lean into a self-development program that calls, I'm unable to predict what will happen.

When I venture where the hostess channels a Council of Twelve, my heart hesitates to speak before asking a clear question.

Today, months past these happenings, I see the events connecting to magnify my journey forward.

Here's the view…by giving up mailings from Publisher's Clearing House, I reign in time handling mail, allowing awareness of other patterns to emerge.

The November program reveals that my attention has been spattered, that I've been afraid of not catching up and that I believed hiding was safe.

These days, I'm more clearly focused, breathing into action without racing, valuing presence with others.

How I live onward from the Council's response offers Michael and me ideas to joyfully create, hugely exciting me.

Hooray!

I've seen time open; I'm more settled within and we have enough ideas to live into for the rest of our days.

This is awesome.

I am more ready than ever to fulfill my soul's purpose to inspire love, peace and joy.

Release an obstacle to your higher calling.

Do You Remember the Hokey Pokey?

Does your memory of the Hokey Pokey give you a reason to smile?

Does your memory have you shaking all about?

Does your memory encourage you to put your whole self in?

Mostly, my memories of the Hokey Pokey revolve around the roller rink, having difficulty with the steps on skates, but loving the part about putting our whole selves in to "Shake it all about."

Years later, I resonate with the Hokey Pokey by noticing how we dabble with life or put our whole selves into play.

Maybe we're spending more time at work than we need to, we're watching more television shows than we'd like or we're eating chips from the bag more often than our waistline appreciates.

If we put our whole selves into life, what changes might we make? Would we set new boundaries at work? Would we release the need to sit in front of so many programs? Would we place our favorite snack into a bowl before sitting down?

Life has taught me that bringing the light of conscious awareness into anything can change everything.

Breathing into awareness can shift a non-working practice into a new approach that works much better.

Illuminate an aspect of life to improve it.

A Few Thoughts on Reverence

Feeling awe in sacred spaces. Speaking quietly on a forest walk. Inhaling the scent of a rose, thanking her afterwards. Allowing others to speak without finishing their sentences. Holding doors open. Not rushing. Moving at the pace of nature. Singing in the key of green. Giving large tips to service workers. Smiling at infants. Petting dogs. Allowing cats to nestle lap-wise. Driving with consideration.

These are a few ways that come to my heart as ways to welcome reverence.

Reverence to me is a feeling of honoring the holy in the ordinary and breathing into a sense of awe in sacred spaces.

I believe practicing reverence engenders kindness, courteousness and gentleness.

I believe reverence brings compassion, admiration and sweet vibrations.

I believe reverence is akin to love communing with all the love there is.

Add a bit of reverence to your days.

On Humble Knees

Have you misplaced your car keys
for the eleventh time? Ached for attention
from a brother incapable of sight
beyond his navel? Navel oranges
come to mind. Winter fruit.
Have you missed strawberries and
plums, tolerated one cloudy day
playing tag with another when all
you wanted to do was hunker down
like your cat inside one yellow square
of sun on the rug?

Did you lose the black leather gloves
you bought on a country road
lined with wisteria outside Florence?
Have you driven sun-spangled hills
of Chianti all day to find a particular vineyard
and almost given up? Then Badia a Coltibuono
appears when you convince your husband
to press on. And you walk past the shop
selling pottery and wine, follow signs to the Abbey,
stand breathing eleventh century air in a holy place
you almost didn't find.

Reconsider Repeating Ways

How many times have we visited the same spot?

Are we used to cooking the same food for annual gatherings?

What might happen if we switch things up?

Wally introduces me to Las Vegas, a town he used to visit with his Dad.

While not a gambler, per se, he enjoys playing 21 when we are on the Strip.

One year, I watch Wally learn a new game, taking his seat when he heads to the ATM.

I fall into a zone of Pai Gow winning hands, one after another.

Joyful.

Future trips to Las Vegas find me happily playing Pai Gow Poker while Wally plays his favorite 21; we meet up later to dine with clients or to see a show.

Years after divorcing, Michael and I visit my older sister and her husband who have moved to Las Vegas; it's the first time Michael's been in this desert town.

While there's an itch inside me (an ego-sized, repeating life itch) to visit the casinos Wally and I used to visit, I quiet these voices inside.

Michael and I instead visit Las Vegas with moment by moment consciousness, just as we visit everywhere we travel.

We turn in at a decent hour, share our morning spiritual practice and enjoy a fabulous meeting with Deb Dorchak, book design diva.

We linger over lunch with my sister and her husband, attend an event where Tea Obreht interviews Terry Tempest Williams and buy tickets my sister suggests, loving the tour of Zappos, Rich Little at the Tropicana and the Neon Museum.

Plus, we enjoy two scrumptious meals following Deb's tip at The Bagel Café and play a few hands of Pai Gow Poker.

Michael and I share my home during COVID-19 sheltering in place, and he amazes me.

His creativity in the kitchen means that NO MEAL is ever the same.

We could eat oatmeal each morning, but no serving would resemble another.

I'm learning that repeating a trip to a town, or a meal we've eaten numerous times can be radically different, interesting and downright wondrous.

May your days offer reasons to shift a pattern.

What can you do differently?

Chapter S

Savoring Seasons in New Ways

Do we attend annual events we adore?
Do we look forward to certain holidays?
Do we notice subtle changes in nature?

Visiting my parents every couple of months in Charlotte, NC, we pass a sign—*Home of the Annual Mallard Creek Presbyterian Church B.B.Q 4th Thursday in October.* Dad says how much he and Mom love it, as I marvel that this spectacle advertises all year for ten hours in the limelight.

Ben comments on nature's annual plays, which feels strange to me, since these events whisk past on fleet feet. How will we wait another year for their return?

Something in me needs to settle down, perhaps, to breathe and to appreciate the ever-flowing manner of life, including annual church events, annual conventions, yearly sales and the annual shedding of leaves, falling snowfall and blooming flowers…cycles we notice, cycles we honor, cycles we miss. Now crocus…soon daffodil…then tulip…an ongoing movement of life unfolding moment to moment, season to season, year to year.

Maybe the trick is to amplify presence to each moment, opening us to a wealth of blessings.

This way, before we blink, autumn returns: I traipse up our back hill embracing a bucket of walnuts while you carve a crazy expression into your pumpkin.

Enter seasons and events with heart.

Practice Self-Care as Non-Negotiable

Self-care.

Perhaps we're running so fast, the term sounds almost comical.

Or maybe we've treated ourselves beautifully for such a long time that we're not even aware we're treating ourselves.

Then again…maybe we're somewhere in between.

Wherever we are is just right.

Awareness enters to move us along, doesn't it?

If we're ready to add a layer of self-care to our routine, what will we add? A massage? Lotion after a shower? An earlier bedtime?

Will we pay more attention to how much water we drink?

Will we buy new water bottles—one for the car and one for our office?

Will we offer our snoring partner a new space for sleep, so our rest can commence with clarity and calm?

Will we clean our closet for easier dressing?

Will we journal our way into additional honoring of ourselves and others?

Will we claim uninterrupted bath time by candlelight?

Will we minimize the amount of caffeine and sugar we ingest?

Will we reach for more raw food, less processed food and less meat?

Will we nurture tucked-away parts of ourselves?

Will we call our friends for heart-to-hearts?

Will we step out to receive a Vitamin D reprieve from fluorescent lights?

Will we walk during lunch to spark our minds, hearts and bodies?

Will we treat ourselves with an apple instead of a cookie?

Add an element of self-care to spark your swagger!

What Separation is Ours to Heal?

Do we feel separate from others?
Do we long for deeper connections with life?
Do we wonder if separation is an illusion?

"Joy, you just don't get it, do you? With you in matter and me with the Power of the Universe, do you see what we can accomplish?" The All (God, Source, Universe…) August 2011.

One August day in 2011, my Pilates instructor compliments my body's alignment on the reformer, and that afternoon, I feel wholly different, as if I'm standing with new power and confidence, newly integrated.

The next night at dinner, conversation between Ben and me is on a spiritual plane above our heads, and I hear myself say that I'm going inward this week.

Sunday morning, I'm given a knowing to clear Ben's low-vibration items from my house.

When I call Ben to share this, he laughs.

"Why are you laughing?" I ask.

"Because, dear, you are so changeable!"

Truly.

As I tell Ben when we meet, "You may not want to get involved with me. I don't know who I am."

Meeting him so soon after my marriage ends, I know I'm not my whole self. I am in a liminal, healing time after the dysfunction of my family growing up and beyond the dynamics of my twenty-seven year marriage to Wally.

Clearing items doesn't feel like I am leaving Ben…only that I need to raise the vibration for this sacred time communing with myself and sacred mystery.

After collecting Ben's slippers, coffee filters and books, I head to church. Surprisingly during meditation, I need to stand seeking comfort, because my ankles and wrists are shocked with energy like never before.

At home, I walk on the grass barefoot, praying to Mother Earth plus all the entities I imagine to mitigate this energy.

Inside, I journal and pray with a sacred box of Angel cards I've treasured for years but rarely entered, crying as I read entries ripe with meanings that resonate to my core.

I play spiritual music.

I sit in silence.

That night, I have trouble sleeping. Energy moves in uncomfortable ways as if it can't find a clearing.

Still feeling poorly in the morning, I draw a bath, seeking relief.

In the tub, I'm visited by a powerful energy called the All, appearing like an unending night sky.

We communicate without words as the All teaches me about compassion, about how powerful I am in matter with the All of space and time within me and that

Separation is an Illusion—I am in the Azalea and the Azalea is in me, I am in the people of Africa and the people of Africa are in me. I am in the All and the All is in me.

Oneness is the only thing in existence.

After the bath, we commune in bed where there's a powerful, orgasmic connection between who I am and the Universe, and where new energy enters my being.

I may forever process the experience while feeling challenged to put words to it, and over time, I've believed different things…that I married God, that my Higher Self came into me and that the Holy Spirit entered my being.

What actually happened appears not to matter as much as the profound effect in my life.

I am given the feeling of BELONGING I've forever longed for.

Processing this feeling of belonging changes the way I walk in the world. I'm more settled into myself. I'm calmer. I'm connected to our loving universe of wisdom and peace.

I belong within.
You belong within.
We belong within.

I belong on the earth.
You belong on the earth.

We belong on the earth.
We belong…we belong…we belong.
We are not separate entities.
We are a part of all that exists.

Have you received a visit from the All, too?

Have you processed the experience with a supportive friend or spiritual companion?

Do you feel separate, or a part of everything?

How does this idea of Separation as an Illusion and Oneness sit with you?

If you would like to talk with a grounded, joyful, spiritual companion, I'd love to listen, offering you love, support and care.

Visit www.joyonyourshoulders.com/contact/ to schedule your confidential, complimentary call.

How Do We Shut Ourselves Down?

Do we tell ourselves it's not worth it to try something new?

Do we live by ignoring desires that arise?

Does a myth or mantra spin that some way or another keeps us stuck?

I mentioned earlier that I spent years hiding in clothes too large with low self-esteem, possibly depressed.

Yep.

I'm not proud of the years I rehashed stories that I wasn't enough, though I love all versions of lil ol' me who did the best I could.

Where do you find your sweet self in this message?

Are you struggling to care for yourself?

Are you taking baby steps forward?

Are you living into a plan to love your whole self?

These days, I'm happily, gratefully evolving into new versions of my Self, inspiring others on the way.

As I understand it, there are zillions of ways to hold ourselves back.

We can listen to loops of negative self-talk or take little responsibility for our lives as we cling to another in co-dependency.

Then there's the way Michael lived, adhering to a

mantra he'd acquired, *Life is easy for those without preferences.*

Michael stagnated in a safe life, for he hadn't allowed his heart's desires to lead him forward…until receiving a wake-up call from the poem *Of Dreams* in this book on page 76.

Did that poem speak to you?

Is it time to turn back to it, and to breathe into it more slowly?

Heaven knows, we're each on an individual journey with a personal schedule, aren't we?

Well, I'm beyond grateful that Michael deeply considered that poem, realizing that he was done living without preferences; he desired to get to know me, and to live into more dreams.

At this writing, we've dated for over two years, and these years have given us more blessings than we could have imagined.

We are a loving, allowing, peace-filled, joy-filled couple without what I call Ego Baloney Bullshit.

We begin and end our days with a spiritual practice, which grounds us into unfolding days we love.

Drama free.

Fun.

Playful.

Inspired.

Supportive.

Thank you, dear Michael, for buying this book, and

for allowing a poem to touch you, awakening you to reach across the divide you'd built.

The ways we play into the unlimited possibilities of life is crazily great.

Live beyond the ways you hold your heart in check.

It turns out that Michael took another step after reading this book; he gathered with a group of awakening souls for a book study, inviting me to attend the last evening.

The study group learned what I know—that this book read and discussed in a circle allows folks to heal, move on and see life in new ways.

Might you gather friends to review this book together?

Snoring and Sleep Apnea

Have we lost sleep due to a snoring partner?

Have we or a loved one tried snoring remedies?

Has anything worked?

Would we categorize these events anywhere in the joyful column?

The most snoring joy I've received involves the creative expression I enjoyed crafting the poem that follows this essay, *The Roaring of Your Snoring in My Sleep-Deprived Ears Blues.*

When my parents live in Ohio, after all three daughters are grown, Mom is diagnosed with mild sleep apnea. Years later, after she crashes a car, breaking her wrist, Mom is diagnosed with severe sleep apnea and dementia, and prescribed a CPap machine.

It's sad to me, while at the same time I understand how this could have happened. Dad is preoccupied with work and life, Mom and Dad sleep in separate bedrooms due to her snoring and my parents forget to revisit the state of Mom's sleep apnea.

My husband's snoring causes me sleepless nights, angst and distress, plus joy allowing *The Roaring of Your Snoring* poem to come through.

He tries *Breathe Right* strips, I try a mattress on the floor in another room and ultimately I retreat to the lower level of the house. Snoring bed partners and I don't match well. How about you?

Dan snored soundly on the other side of the house.

Before the pandemic of 2020, Michael slept at his place, spending weekends under my roof. Am I ever grateful that he doesn't snore, enabling us to share covers. He's also a dream, allowing me to steal blankets without complaining.

Nothing engenders more joy in any of us, perhaps, than getting a good night's rest.

Happy sleep, everyone!

May we receive deep sleep.

The Roaring of Your Snoring In My Sleep-Deprived Ears Blues

Something's shifted in our marriage,
More than weight around a middle.
Your nightly sounds invade my
Beauty sleep more than a little.

Windows rattle with this drama,
One slick motor's in your chest
Humming overtime all night when
I could snatch some priceless rest.

I wake up scads of blessed times
To poke you like you said,
But peaceful sleep's elusive
Tossing me across our bed.

Morning enters, oh so swiftly,
Yellowed eyes reveal the fight.
Normal clarity is absent,
My feelings wound so tight.

There was a time I longed to have
You off the road back home.
Now I say, "Dear, hit the streets—
Let me snare my zzzz's alone!"

Support Hugely Matters

Have we felt supported in life?
Have we offered rich support to others?
What does the topic bring up inside you?

As you likely gathered from earlier essays, I didn't grow up feeling emotionally supported by my family.

Mom mostly picked me up late from school events, my older sister repeatedly told me I didn't belong and Dad insisted we eat in silence, since the nightly news was on.

Okay.

Support.

I honestly didn't truly understand the idea until the last couple of years.

Snorkeling in the waters of Kauai, the retreat leader stops to check on me, just as I'm ready to abort.

"How's it going, Joy? Are your goggles leaking?"

I say that they are, that I'm cold and that I've had enough of this first-time snorkeling adventure.

"Here, try mine, and hang in there; you're super close to seeing the sea turtles."

Wow.

Support.

I feel supported to carry on…to go a little further…to not retreat.

When I return from Kauai, a card is waiting for me from Michael, which pierces my heart with goodness.

I realize, too, that Michael and his grandson offered tremendous support when I moved from Ben's house.

And that he'd invited me to attend a book circle of THIS VERY BOOK as the author for their last night potluck, paying me to show up.

Support.

With Michael as partner, I'm finally learning what it's truly like to give and receive support.

Magical.

Beautiful.

Just right.

To all the support you give and receive.

Synchronicity—Our Peek into Mystery

Are you familiar with this word some use for serendipity or coincidence?

Have you experienced this in ways that boggle your mind?

Does it increase your sense of Oneness?

When a new acquaintance asks where I live, I reply that I live in synchronicity. She often says she lives there too, and we laugh with shared understanding. Isn't it the best?

Honestly, I adore those times when an incident or interior message, dream or prayer is reflected back to me.

Enjoy a few notes from my storehouse of synchronicities:

The wallpaper shown in the Home Sweet Home cross stitch kit I open in 1981 matches the wallpaper in the kitchen of the home we've just moved into.

Driving the winding road to a writing workshop, I receive a knowing I'll run into someone I know. Before the next day's session on *Writing from the Body*, a nearby woman catches my attention, saying I look familiar to her. I look her way.

"You're my high school English teacher!"

Elma rushes over for a hug.

Wow. It's been over twenty-five years.

What a wonderful gift to re-connect, plus we stay in touch, enriching one another's lives.

I wake up on Valentine's Day knowing I'll receive a miracle. Two hours later, Uncle Harvey calls, a singular, odd and marvelous experience. The poem I write after his call follows this essay.

While my son and his girlfriend travel in Vietnam during wide travels from their German home, I meet a veteran of the Vietnam War named Dan, and Dan and my son also have the same birthday, which strikes me as highly synchronistic, a sign that this connection is meant to be.

We start dating.

Soon, Dan begins living with Ben and me, and their fast friendship grows beyond imagining.

Is this my life?

To all the synchronicities we can treasure.

Uncle Harvey

I

You are mom's only sibling,
her big brother who builds radios, loves opera,
the one who lights her night sky with stars.

As a young man, you join ROTC,
find yourself on active duty in a foxhole
where your brain waves crash in tumult.

Institutionalized, medicated, isolated.

Mom's parents tell her to sail far away,
to float a happy life, not to tie a rock
around her ankle and jump overboard.

She sinks anyway.

I think she stows you away, holds you
bone to bone until she indents her soul
with boulder-sized guilt.

2

As a little girl when I ask about you,
mom's stormy answers keep me quiet.
I stop casting your name out loud

but I continue to drop lines.

On Valentine's Day in my 45th year,
you surface by phone, tell me
you've saved all 18 of my letters.

I float on the waves of your voice,
sit down to pen my 19th letter to you.

Chapter T,U

Who Knew…
Our Thoughts Have Power

Do we understand how much our thoughts create our lives?

Do we see that what's not working is a result of us being who we are?

Can we evolve into thinking of a higher quality?

I'm not sure that I fully understood this amazing concept until a day last summer.

Here's the view…

Michael and I enjoy a wondrous trip to Germany surrounding my younger son's wedding.

We land early in Xanten to adjust to the time

change and to honor my birthday, make our way to Greve to join family for the wedding and travel by train down the Rhine. These blue-sky vacation days enable us to savor gelato strolls, breathe beside fountains and treasure moments.

Months earlier when we'd purchased tickets, returning to western North Carolina didn't work out, so we find ourselves landing in Charleston, South Carolina on a hot, muggy night.

We're the last ones through customs, weary owners of a wayward bag that doesn't arrive.

Hmm…okay.

A short way from the airport, our rental car makes a crazy sound, to which Michael says, "It sounds like this car's falling apart. We'd better exchange it."

It's no fun crossing the hot parking lot this hot night dressed in long pants and long sleeves from flying, but it is what it is; we manage without whining.

We use the restroom, receive a replacement car and head out again.

And…when we locate our Air BnB, the entry code doesn't work.

Oh, my.

What is going on? Three things have gone awry tonight.

This feels strange, especially since our trip to Germany overflowed with ease, fun and laughter.

We long to be inside air conditioning and to sleep.

Thankfully, a few minutes later, we hear from the Air BnB folks that it didn't work to set the code they'd given us. "Use this one, instead."

Hooray!

We enter the cool, lovely home, soon finding our way to sleep after the long flights and trying moments in Charleston.

The next morning as we walk to breakfast, Michael fesses up, "I'm sorry things were wonky last night, Joy. I held energy of not wanting to be home."

OMG.

"NO WONDER we experienced a crazy evening with things going wrong. Michael; you're a powerful manifester!!!"

Yes.

We create our lives.

We live in ease and flow, or we don't.

What thoughts are we thinking?

May our thoughts offer goodness to our days.

Joyful Truths to Touch Upon

Life is fleeting.
Embrace life one moment at a time.
Sit quietly breathing.
Laugh every day.
Love.
Kindness matters.
Being peaceful brings peace where we wander.
Time with friends adds music to our song.
Being matters. Doing matters.
Being joyful rocks.
May we have all we desire.
May we share with abandon.
May we engage deeply with life.

Chapter V

How Visible Can We Be with Our Gifts?

What does the word ***visible*** *bring up in us?*
Are we comfortable with invisibility?
Is it time to shed a layer of invisibility?
What gifts can we share with others, and what are we waiting for?

Let's enter a bit of light if we've been hiding in shadow.

Test the waters. See if you can feel a sense of rightness in this new place. Then test again in a new setting. See how your acceptance of being visible makes visibility possible.

Admittedly, visibility is a newer practice for me. I

lean into one action at a time. First, I write a few posts; next, I post them on my website. I begin a newsletter for subscribers; I offer joyful wares in unfamiliar venues.

Visibility to me is another way to say we believe in ourselves—we belong everywhere taking up space, sharing our gifts, allowing our lights to shine.

Who among us hasn't heard the song about not hiding our light in a barrel?

We are created as light-bearing beings, radiant, energetic souls who enlighten others.

May we allow our unique gifts to shimmer.

Chapter W

Joyful Wares to Share

Radiant creations shine on a hook, though I'm reluctant to release them.

The next day, a friend happens by the café where I'm eating lunch, allowing me to spill a couple cranky thoughts about control and creativity. Don's happy to follow me home to see what I've created, where his seasoned words heal layers of fear about untethered creations.

With new freedom to move ahead, I decide that Sunday is a stellar day to cross my rental's threshold wearing a creation that says *Make an appointment with joy*. Stepping out the door, I pause as my ego pipes up, "What do you think you're doing? Who do you think you are?"

Sigh.

Swiftly, my Higher Self responds that I've been waiting my whole life for this moment.

Off I go wearing an inspired creation, knowing I'll receive praise and criticism. Just as we don't like everything we encounter, radiant creations worn like a minister's stole will attract and repel, speak and not speak.

This is the path.

I visit stores, attend craft fairs and receive invitations to network. Sales and joyful receptions offer affirmation. I wear creations like a uniform, and tote a satchel of stoles for interested buyers.

Customers ask for new words and phrases, expanding the list. Yes to *Peace, Love* and *Joy*. Yes to *Comfort Ye, Grace* and *Serenity.*

A new seamstress asks, "What do I do with this bag filled with small pieces of fabric?"

"Let's make small wares."

We create bookmarks and *Portable Joy* to adorn purses, backpacks, wine bottles and more.

At a women's workshop, Heather makes a suggestion.

"Joy, since you have two chocolate expressions and since I love giving gourmet chocolate bars to friends, it'd be great if you could offer candy bags."

And we do.

Carolyn answers a J.O.Y.S. ad for seamstresses, telling me she needs to make x dollars per hour.

An earlier version of me would have felt rattled, stammering or hanging up. This version replies from a deeper place before my programmed mind kicks in.

"How fast can you sew?"

At a November 2013 craft fair, I'm given a postcard to become a vendor at a large event in December. Googling it after dinner, I see that it costs much more than I've paid, it lasts three days instead of one and I ask myself if I'm ready for an event of this nature.

The answer arriving within assures me, "Yes, with sewing support, you absolutely are ready."

A call to Carolyn confirms her role to sew and sew.

After two days at the larger venue, a new belief dawns…*I belong anywhere with these inspired wares.*

The following day, I receive an email inviting me to vend at The Spiritual Directors International (SDI) Conference in Santa Fe, New Mexico.

This feels synchronistic with my new understanding. Additionally, I'm certified in spiritual direction, I've been interested in traveling to the southwest and I'd like to see how conventions differ from craft fairs.

No doubt. I'm meant to attend the SDI Conference in April.

Before the first day of the Santa Fe conference ends, Catholic women prohibited from ordination tell me their stories through tears of joy with this chance to buy and wear my stoles.

What a beautiful surprise.

And new understandings of my wares unfold and unfold.

A woman slips prayer beads into a candy bag that says *Blessings*. Another celebrates the perfect cases she finds for sunglasses and sacred stones. A man tests the fit of his cell phone in a bag that says *Balance*.

Myriad souls gaze into my eyes, thanking me for bringing Divinity into the material world.

Hugs abound, and I shed tears of gratitude and exhaustion. Vendors say my being and wares belong at other events they name, sending me further into the world.

At The Unity Peoples Convention in June, a nearby vendor plays gorgeous music all day. When I have a chance to visit, Jay introduces a CD by Faerie Elaine Silver, which includes a beautiful poem he birthed called *Yes, I Understand.*

I repeatedly listen to this CD at home and in my car, and a few weeks later, I notice on Facebook that Elaine will present at The Namaste Center in Hendersonville, North Carolina.

How great!

I'll have the opportunity to be with this soulful singer/songwriter in a nearby place I've been meaning to visit.

Elaine's appearance coincides with a regional meeting of the Alliance of Divine Love (ADL), inspiring me to become an ADL minister. ADL is a nondenominational ministry whose ministers offer The Greatest Degree of Love, officiate at weddings and other ceremonies and open spiritual centers.

Attending the first potluck gathering of The Namaste Center, I meet Dan, an answer to my heart's desire to share moments with an engaging, adventuresome soul.

At my first ADL convention Divine/Love stoles are widely purchased, and I learn about a Healing Touch convention in Naples, Florida in October.

See you on the road!

Follow inspiration on its adventurous journey.

A Few Words about Water

Are we drinking enough water?
Are we aware how important water is to our health?

Water.

Grab your water bottle, and then return; hydrate well before reading this essay to receive its most complete benefit.

I'm teasing, kind of.

Seriously, if you need a drink, take a break to get one; I'm a tad sensitive to the idea that we drink enough water.

Growing up, underweight me thinks water fills me up, so I won't be able to eat the next meal.

Yikes. I'm seriously misinformed.

You're right.

I pay a price for not hydrating with body issues we won't name. Suffice it to say, I suffer plenty, leading to my current practices with H2O. Yep, my water bottles and I bond like new friends at a shoe sale or a ball game.

We've all heard we're made of 60% or more water with a quantity of daily ounces we require. I'm not such a numbers woman, but life has taught me that our skin, energy and sleep all work better when we drink water throughout the day.

Our kidneys prefer it. Our brains desire it. Our hearts require it. Our skin loves it. Water, water. Lift a cup for healthy living!

Swallow sensational sips of water.

The Way of Mastery

List several of your favorite books.
Do you notice a pattern?
Are you surprised?

In 2015, Dan and I enjoy a friend's picnic in Asheville, North Carolina where I meet a woman who invites me to a circle in her home.

The first time attending, I learn that each woman knows a book I've never heard of called *The Way of Mastery.*

Since I've long adored reading spiritual texts that support my evolution, I order a copy.

OMG.

I treasure the messages in this book published by the Shanti Christo Foundation (www.shantichristo.com).

So far, I've daily read and reread passages for five years, sharing word of this book with soul sisters and packing it for road trips.

When Michael and I begin dating in 2018, he asks for advice to start a spiritual practice; before we know it, *The Way of Mastery* enters our morning calls.

Jeshua's channeled words are beautiful and rich, leading us into consciousness conversations, deeply changing us.

Here's a taste of the book's Introduction:

You hold in your hands the treasured teachings of Jeshua ben Joseph (Jesus), one of the greatest Masters humankind has ever known. These teachings were given during the years 1994–1997. Please do not hurry as you read through each lesson. Rather, allow each sentence to be held within the heart, each idea to fill the mind and the body with its very real frequency and vibration. For each word, the structure of each sentence, the cadence and the humor, is by design.

These words are to be studied and savored over and over, until their meaning deepens and flowers into the grace of Christ living in you and as you, allowing the ray of that Light to penetrate your mind, correcting every perception you have ever held about yourself or the world…

And your life will begin to be guided by a Voice that is not your own until the voice you have called your own is no longer heard. What has been called the ego will simply dissolve, and the mind will know perfect peace.

Does this take time? You are as close as the choice to teach only Love…May you be transformed by The Way of Mastery in your unique process of remembering who you really are.

Consider taking a look at this book.

X
Y
Z

Chapter X, Y, Z

Zebras, Of Course

The way I understand it, no alphabetical book is complete without Zebras.

Anyway, just thinking about striped zebras makes me smile.

You, too? Fun!

Next my mind goes to patterns in animals, which leads me to consider Tigers…Leopards…Giraffes…which brings me to imagine limitless designs in nature…

Rings of life in tree stumps. Rose petals unfolding. Daisy petals to claim love, or not. Crabapple branches to climb. Lilac bushes to race to. Buckeyes to collect. Puppies to pet. Walnuts to harvest. Daylilies to shine.

The blessings of nature arrive down so many avenues.

Are we receiving them?
Are we stepping out of our homes?
Are we taking walks?

Celebrate the gifts of nature!

Live with Zest

If we were to live with zest, what would we do differently?

Would we watch less television?
Would we attend additional live events?
Would we try fresh restaurants?
Would we visit newfangled places?

While joy was squashed in my family of origin, there also was a ZEST for living.

Zest expresses through Dad's desire to dine deliciously…from Sunday lox and bagels to dinner at The Spinning Wheel, from Liederkranz cheese to Kringle.

Zest arrives through Mom's mini-cheesecake squares gussied up for guests.

Zest brings vacations to Mt. Rushmore, to a rodeo and on a houseboat.

Zest finds us cruising the Atlantic on The Sea Venture and The Oceanic.

Zest scores music lessons, magazine subscriptions and Broadway shows.

Zest translates into concerts, museums and art lessons.

Zest sends show tunes through the living room speakers.

Zest takes trips to three grocery stores for weekly specials…oh, my.

To all the zest we can muster!

Acknowledgements

Thank you to my Ancestors, who honor me each day, widely guiding this book into the world. Bless you for gracing little girl me with hugs, cozy laps and sparkling eyes above tricky false teeth.

Thank you to the creative team of Wendi Kelly and Deb Dorchak! You crafted an amazing logo for *Joy on Your Shoulders,* a gorgeous website and held my heart and hands through book after book, including this second edition, with all the wisdom, care and love you are. I respect you, cherish you and love you, dear Wendi and Deb.

Thank you to my parents, Glenn and Gladys, to my sisters Lynn and Ellen, and to my life partners, Wally, Ben, Dan and Michael.

Andrew and Kevin, thank you for being the wonderful, talented, adventuresome young adults you are, and for all the joy we share. May your lives with Jaime Lyn and Anna be wondrous beyond your imaginings, and may we visit as we're able.

To former and current *Joy on Your Shoulders* seamstresses who brought light and inspiration through your skills and sweetness in your characters, Gail, Joy, Cheryl, Janice, Carolyn, Carolyn, Ray, Jessica, Lauren, Solange, Nancy, Anne, and Ardith.

To my awesome, unrepeatable friends, including, but not limited to Rita, Susie, Lori, Jessica, Randy, Ellie,

Kelly, Marie, Alyce t., Emilie, Kathy, Connie, Linda, Mary, Donna, Elise, Barbara Jean, Polly, Catherine, Emily, Kara and Gladys Petey, I love and appreciate each one of you more than I let you know.

To those who gathered Monday mornings in northeastern Ohio to study *A Course in Miracles* with me, thank you for engaging, questioning and explaining. Thank you for your hugs and comfy couches.

To early readers of this manuscript, thank you for your time, feedback and affirmation. You include Charlotte, John, Chelsea, Suka, Craig, Mary Margaret, Diana, Sierra, Kevin, Anna, Donna, Stacie, Anne and others I may have missed naming—thank you, too.

And thank each one of you, named and unnamed, who've exchanged words, support and energy with me along the way. You matter. You're enough. You're golden.

Author photo by Michelle Citrin

About the Author

Joy writes inspiring books in western North Carolina. She's an Alliance of Divine Love Minister, certified in spiritual direction and founder of *Joy on Your Shoulders*, where she inspires love, peace and joy through her being, through Batik wares sewn by local seamstresses, through a free newsletter that goes to subscribers and through all the ways she evolves to connect with you. Taking breaks from the computer, Joy hoops in sunbeams.

www.joyonyourshoulders.com

CPSIA information can be obtained
at www.ICGtesting.com
Printed in the USA
LVHW050750130721
692514LV00001B/14

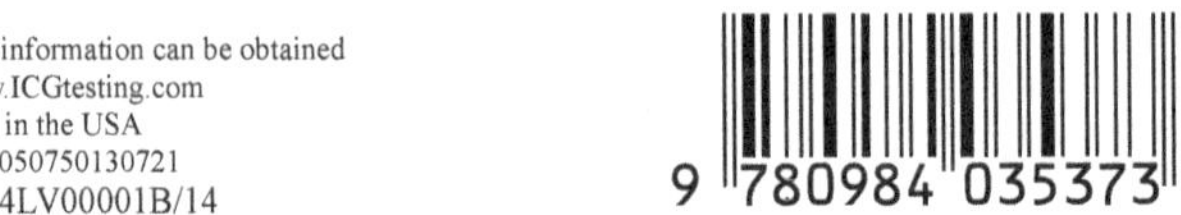

9 780984 035373